Just Married
COOKBOOK

Presented To

_____

By

_____

Just Married
COOKBOOK

by

Ruth Gessler & Sandy Stasko

First Printing, March 1994
Second Printing, March 1995

ISBN 1-55056-294-0

Canadian Cataloguing in Publication Data

Gessler, Ruth
Just married cookbook

Includes index.

1.Cookery for two. I.Stasko, Sandy II.Title
TX652.G47 1994   641.5'61   C94-910246-6

Cover Art Work by
Vo ' kel Designs
Wendee L. Cote & Sandra H. Willems

Photography by
SanRu

Published by
Just Married Publishing
P.O. Box 431, Station M
Calgary, Alberta, Canada T2P 2J1

Printed in Canada

DEDICATION

This book is dedicated:

to our husbands *Ray* and *Mike* for their encouragement and support, and for tasting and tasting and tasting;

to *Matthew*, *Zachary* and *Elizabeth* who will need this book when they set up their own households someday;

and to *God* who created the food sources from which these recipes were derived.

To Our Readers,

*We hope you enjoy the recipes in **Just Married Cookbook** as much as we do and would like to hear from you if you have any questions or comments.*

All recipes in this unique book have been tested by the conventional method and rounded metric equivalents given. For those who would like a more exact measurement in metric, a conversion chart is located on page 13, showing both the exact metric conversions and the conversions used in this book.

The meals suggested are for the average person. Those with specific nutritional needs should consult a physician to make sure those needs are met.

*To aid in grocery purchasing, **Going Shopping** lists may be copied for **your own personal use**.*

If the order form has been removed, please let us know and we will supply you with one.

We wish you the best in your cooking adventures.

Ruth and Sandy

Just Married Cookbook
P.O. Box 431, Station M
Calgary, Alberta, Canada T2P 2J1

TABLE OF CONTENTS

BEFORE YOU BEGIN   8

STOCKING THE SHELVES
  Equipment   10
  Household Needs   12
  Staples   12

USEFUL INFORMATION
  Metric Conversion   13
  Equivalents   14
  Terms   14

MONTH OF MEALS
  Week 1   19
  Week 2   37
  Week 3   55
  Week 4   73

SWEET THINGS   91

SOMETHING SPECIAL
  Anniversary   111
  Birthday   115
  Christmas   121
  Coffee & Dessert   127
  Easter   133
  Thanksgiving   137
  Valentine's Day   143

INDEX   149

BEFORE YOU BEGIN

Just Married Cookbook

♦ Is designed for the novice or experienced cook to use.

♦ Contains:

- a month of suggested meals, that are interesting and varied, to save meal planning time;

- delicious recipes that can easily be interchanged to create other meals;

- recipes that have been fully tested, designed to serve two average appetites;

- special recipes, designed in six generous portions, for holidays and special events when family or friends are invited;

- shopping guides to aid in grocery purchases, with amounts shown in conventional measurements and rounded to metric.

- wedding customs and quips for your entertainment.

♦ Works best when you:

- carefully read through the recipes before you begin - when preparing an entire meal, you may need to work on more than one recipe at a time;

- assemble all utensils and ingredients before you start, to make sure you have everything you need;

- check the progress of your cooking before the specified time - ovens, equipment, etc. can affect the timing.

- clean as you work - have a sink filled with water to rinse utensils and to soak stubborn pans;

- experiment with different brands - flavors and consistency may vary.

♦ Helps with entertaining when you:

- follow the suggested preparation timetables;

- prepare some foods beforehand such as desserts and salads, but be sure to refrigerate any foods that might spoil;

- have coffee and water measured and in the coffee maker, ready to turn on;

- set serving dishes out on the counter to speed up last minute serving;

- begin serving your guests with cold dishes such as salads, and then hot dishes, to help keep hot foods from getting cool before eating.

STOCKING THE SHELVES

EQUIPMENT (used in *Just Married Cookbook*)

broiling pan with rack

cake pans:
  non-stick bundt, non-stick heart shaped, non-stick mini fruit cake pan,
  springform - 9 x 2¾ inches (22 x 7 cm), square - 8 inch (20 cm)

can opener

coffee maker

colander

cookie sheet with edges, non-stick - 15¼ x 10¼ x ¾ inches (38.7 x 26.3 x 1.9 cm)

covered casseroles:
  small - 1½ qt (1.5 L), medium - 2 qt (2 L), large - 3 qt (3 L)

covered saucepans:
  small - 1 qt (1 L), medium - 2 qt (2 L), large - 4 qt (4 L)

6 dessert dishes - 1 cup (250 mL)

dishes:
  setting for 6, including gravy boat, small and large salad bowls, platter,
  vegetable bowls

frying pan:
  small - 8 inches (20 cm), large - 11 inches (28 cm)

grater

kitchen shears

measuring cups

measuring spoons

meat thermometer

mixer

mixing bowls, glass or metal:
  small, medium, large

muffin tin, non-stick - 12 unit

oven mitts

2 oven-proof quiche dishes - 6 x 1½ inches (15 x 3.8 cm)

2 oven-proof ramekins - 1 cup (250 mL)

2 parfait glasses

pie plate, non-stick - 9 x 1¼ inches (22.9 x 3.23 cm)

pizza pan, non-stick

roasting pan - 13 x 8 x 5 inches (33 x 20 x 13 cm)

set of cutlery including 2 long spoons and carving set

4 skewers - 9 inches (23 cm)

6 tall glasses

utensils:
  melon scoop, pancake turner, pastry brush, potato masher, rubber spatula, slotted spoons, vegetable peeler, wire whisk, wooden picks and spoons

water pitcher

EQUIPMENT (nice to have)

barbecue

chocolate fondue set

chopsticks

cooling rack

scale

splatter screen

steak knives

warming tray

HOUSEHOLD NEEDS
foil
non-stick cooking spray
paper towels
plastic wrap
toothpicks

STAPLES
baking supplies
bread and crackers
butter and/or margarine
chips
coffee and tea
convenience mixes
honey and syrup
jams and jellies
juices
ketchup
mayonnaise
milk
mixes (pancake mix, etc.)
mustard
nuts
oil
pastas
pickled foods
relish
rice
salad dressings
salt and pepper
sauces
seasonings
shortening
spices
sugars
vinegar

USEFUL INFORMATION

METRIC CONVERSION

Conventional	Metric Conversion (exact)	Metric Conversion (used in this book)
Spoons:		
⅛ tsp	.6 mL	.6 mL
¼ tsp	1.2 mL	1.2 mL
½ tsp	2.4 mL	2.5 mL
1 tsp	4.7 mL	5 mL
1 tbsp	14.2 mL	15 mL
Cups:		
¼ cup	56.8 mL	60 mL
⅓ cup	75.6 mL	85 mL
½ cup	113.7 mL	125 mL
⅔ cup	151.2 mL	165 mL
¾ cup	170.5 mL	185 mL
1 cup	227.3 mL	250 mL
1 qt	946.3 mL	1 L
Ounces:		
¼ oz	7.1 g	7 g
⅓ oz	9.4 g	9 g
½ oz	14.2 g	14 g
1 oz	28.3 g	28 g
2 oz	56.7 g	57 g
3 oz	85 g	85 g
4 oz	113.4 g	114 g
5 oz	141.7 g	142 g
6 oz	170.1 g	170 g
7 oz	198.4 g	198 g
8 oz	226.8 g	227 g
16 oz	453.6 g	454 g

EQUIVALENTS (used in this book)

3 tsp	=	1 tbsp	15 mL
4 tbsp	=	¼ cup	60 mL
2 cups	=	1 pint	500 mL
2 pints	=	1 quart	1 L
8 oz	=	½ lb	227 g
16 oz	=	1 lb	454 g
36 oz	=	2¼ lbs	1 kg

TERMS

Beat	Brisk whipping motion.
Blend	Mix two or more ingredients until smooth.
Boil	Bubbles come to the surface and break.
Broil	To place food on a broiler that sears and cooks it - thick cuts should be cooked further away from the heat at a slightly lower temperature.
Chill	Refrigerate.
Chop	Cut food in pieces about the size of peas.
Coat	To sprinkle food with, or dip it into, oil, chips, etc., until covered.
Cool	Remove from heat and let stand at room temperature.
Cream	Beat until smooth.
Dash	A small amount, less than ⅛ tsp (.6 ml).
Dice	To cut into very small pieces, about ¼" (6 mm)
Dollop	Lump.

Fluff	To make light and soft.
Garnish	To decorate with pieces of contrasting food.
Grate	To rub food on a grater in order to produce fine, medium or coarse particles.
Kabob	Cubes of meat, poultry or vegetables for placing on a skewer.
Marinate	To soak in a marinade to give flavor or make tender.
Mince	To chop or cut into very small pieces.
Pare	To cut off outside skin, as from an apple or potato.
Pinch	A very small amount held between the thumb and index finger.
Pulp	Fleshy part of fruit or a vegetable.
Ramekin	An individual baking dish.
Saute	Fry lightly in a little butter or margarine or other fat.
Shred	To cut into slivers or slender pieces.
Simmer	Cook in liquid at a low temperature, just below boiling.
Toss	To mix ingredients lightly with a lifting motion, using 2 forks or spoons.
Warm Oven	200°F (100°C)
Whip	To beat rapidly to increase volume through the incorporation of air.

THERE ARE MANY WAYS TO SAY "I LOVE YOU"

COOKING IS A WONDERFUL WAY!

PICNIC

HOBOS, page 30
GARDEN SALAD, page 30
ANTS ON A LOG, page 31

LOOKING IT OVER

WEEK 1

MONDAY
Crunchy Chicken
Parsley Potatoes
Fruit Bowl

TUESDAY
Spaghetti
Meat Sauce

WEDNESDAY
Veal Kabobs
Steamed Rice

THURSDAY
Ham and Potato Casserole
Carrot/Raisin Salad

FRIDAY
Salmon Scramble
Honeydew Melon Slices
Buttered Toast

SATURDAY
Hobos
Garden Salad
Ants On A Log

SUNDAY
Turkey Roll-ups
Acorn Squash
Nectarine Wedges

COOKING IT UP

So easy! While potatoes and chicken are baking, make the salad and chill - then put up your feet and relax.

PARSLEY POTATOES

2	2	medium red potatoes
2 tbsp	30 mL	butter or margarine
¼ cup	60 mL	sour cream
½ tsp	2.5 mL	parsley flakes

- Preheat oven to 400°F (200°C).
- Scrub potatoes and cut in 8 - 10 slices; spread out slices (for faster cooking) on 2 pieces of well-greased foil and wrap.
- Bake 50 minutes or until tender.
- In a small saucepan, over medium heat, melt butter or margarine; remove from heat and combine with sour cream and parsley flakes.
- To serve potatoes, remove from foil and top with sour cream mixture.

CRUNCHY CHICKEN

2	2	boneless, skinless chicken breasts
3 tbsp	45 mL	vegetable oil
⅔ cup	165 mL	crushed regular potato chips

- Preheat oven to 400°F (200°C).
- Cut chicken breasts in half and dip in oil.
- Coat with chips.
- Place on foil lined cookie sheet and bake 35 - 40 minutes or until meat loses its pink color inside.
- Serve hot.

P.S.
Cooked chicken is needed for recipes during the next three weeks. It may be cooked at this time (don't cover with chips). Slice or chop cooked chicken in required amounts according to future recipes; freeze.

FRUIT BOWL

10 oz	284 mL	canned diced fruit salad, drained
½ cup	125 mL	miniature fruit marshmallows
3 tbsp	45 mL	colored fancy coconut
2 tbsp	30 mL	mayonnaise

- In a small mixing bowl, combine all ingredients.
- Cover with plastic wrap and chill, at least 15 minutes, until ready to serve.

P.S.
Whipped cream or a blend of mayonnaise and sour cream make delicious substitutes for the mayonnaise in this salad.

GOING SHOPPING

12½ oz	355 g	boneless, skinless chicken breasts
10 oz	284 mL	canned diced fruit salad
2	2	red potatoes (medium)
2 oz	60 mL	sour cream

Check Your Shelves For:
butter or margarine
colored fancy coconut
mayonnaise
miniature fruit marshmallows
parsley flakes
regular potato chips
vegetable oil

P.S.
*If making extra chicken for recipes during the next four weeks, remember to increase **Going Shopping** amounts.*

COOKING IT UP

MEAT SAUCE

This recipe does double duty - first it's part of an Italian meal and then with just a few more ingredients, it becomes a favorite Spanish dish.

1 lb	454 g	lean ground beef
¼ cup	60 mL	chopped onion
¼ cup	60 mL	chopped green pepper
1 tsp	5 mL	basil leaves
1 tsp	5 mL	seasoning salt
1 tsp	5 mL	pureed garlic
14 oz	398 mL	canned stewed tomatoes, drained
14 oz	398 mL	canned tomato sauce
4	4	medium mushrooms, sliced
(optional)		grated Parmesan cheese

- In a medium saucepan, over medium/high heat, cook ground beef and onion, stirring frequently, for 7 minutes or until meat loses its pink color.
- Add remaining ingredients, except cheese, reduce heat to medium and continue cooking, stirring occasionally, for another 5 minutes.
- To serve, spoon *half the meat sauce over pasta.
- If desired, sprinkle with Parmesan cheese before serving.

** Freeze the remaining meat sauce to make **Planned Over Chili**, see Thursday - Week 4, page 80.*

P.S.
Juices drained from vegetables can be saved for soup stocks.

LOVE HALVES OUR HARDSHIPS
AND DOUBLES OUR DELIGHT.

SPAGHETTI

2 tsp	10 mL	salt
2 qt	2 L	hot water
7 oz	198 g	spaghetti
1 tbsp	15 mL	butter or margarine

- In a large saucepan, over medium/high heat, bring salted water to a boil.
- Spaghetti may be broken in half for easier handling; stir into boiling water.
- Cook, stirring frequently, for 7 - 9 minutes or until tender; drain.
- Toss with butter or margarine to prevent pasta from sticking; top with meat sauce (previous page) and serve.

P.S.
To tell if spaghetti is ready, throw it against the wall (it sticks when done). For the more conservative: taste the spaghetti - it should be soft, but not mushy.

GOING SHOPPING

14 oz	398 mL	canned stewed tomatoes
14 oz	398 mL	canned tomato sauce
2 oz	57 g	green pepper
1 lb	454 g	lean ground beef
4	4	mushrooms (medium)
2 oz	57 g	onion

Check Your Shelves For:
basil leaves
butter or margarine
grated Parmesan cheese (optional)
pureed garlic
salt
seasoning salt
spaghetti

COOKING IT UP

Begin this meal by marinating the veal. Next, start cooking the rice and then prepare vegetables for the skewers.

VEAL KABOBS

16	16	veal kabobs
1	1	small onion, cut into 12 wedges
8	8	cherry tomatoes
1	1	large green pepper, seeds removed and cut into 12 wedges
8	8	small mushrooms

- Marinate veal (below).
- Preheat broiler if manufacturer directs.
- When meat is marinated, string on four 9" (23 cm) skewers, alternating 2 vegetables with each kabob, beginning and ending with vegetables.
- Put prepared skewers on a cookie sheet and place sheet 6" (15 cm) from source of heat.
- Broil, turning once or twice, for 12 - 15 minutes or until meat loses its pink color inside.
- Serve on a bed of Steamed Rice.

MARINADE

4 tsp	20 mL	beef marinade
½ cup	125 mL	cold water

- In a small mixing bowl, combine beef marinade and water; blend thoroughly.
- Add the veal kabobs and marinate 15 minutes, turning kabobs several times.

P.S.
For easier vegetable and meat removal, wipe skewers with vegetable oil before using.

STEAMED RICE

1 cup	250 mL	hot water
¼ tsp	1.2 mL	salt
2 tsp	10 mL	butter or margarine
½ cup	125 mL	natural long grain rice

- In a small saucepan, over medium heat, combine water, salt and butter or margarine and bring to a boil.
- Add rice, cover tightly, reduce heat to low and simmer 20 minutes or until water is absorbed.
- Remove from heat and let stand covered for 5 minutes.
- Fluff with a fork before serving.

MARRIAGE IS THE CUP THAT
HOLDS THE NECTAR OF LOVE.

GOING SHOPPING

½ oz	14 g	beef marinade
8	8	cherry tomatoes
1	1	green pepper (large)
8	8	mushrooms (small)
1	1	onion (small)
1 lb	454 g	veal kabobs

Check Your Shelves For:
butter or margarine
natural long grain rice
salt

P.S.
If veal kabobs are not available, you can purchase veal loin chops and cut into kabobs.

COOKING IT UP

HAM AND POTATO CASSEROLE

2¾ oz	78 g	scalloped potatoes mix [1 cup (250 mL) potato flakes and 2½ tbsp (37.5 mL) sauce mix]
1 cup	250 mL	water
⅓ cup	85 mL	condensed cream of broccoli soup
⅓ cup	85 mL	milk
1¼ cups	310 mL	chopped smoked cooked ham
1 cup	250 mL	grated mild cheddar cheese

- Preheat oven to 400°F (200°C).
- In a small greased casserole, combine potato flakes and sauce mix.
- In a small saucepan, over medium heat, stirring frequently, bring water, soup and milk to a boil.
- Pour soup mixture over potatoes, mix well and bake 25 minutes.
- Spread with ham, sprinkle with cheese and continue baking 15 minutes longer or until potatoes are fork-tender.
- Cool slightly before serving.

P.S.
Leftover cream of broccoli soup may be frozen for future casserole use.

DID YOU KNOW?

Giving gifts to bridesmaids probably began as a ransom payment back in the 18th century. When the wedding supper was over and the groom came to claim his bride, her maids would first take him to a woman hidden behind a curtain - the bride's grandmother. Next they would lead him to a veiled woman who was really an older aunt. In desperation, the groom would offer a gift of money for the real bride and then she would be brought to him.

CARROT/RAISIN SALAD

The color and flavor of this salad makes it a wonderful compliment to any meal.

1 cup	250 mL	grated carrots
2 tbsp	30 mL	golden seedless raisins
2 tsp	10 mL	granulated sugar
2 tbsp	30 mL	mayonnaise
1 tsp	5 mL	milk

- In a small mixing bowl, combine all ingredients; mix well.
- Cover with plastic wrap and chill at least 20 minutes, until ready to serve.

GOING SHOPPING

5 oz	142 g	carrots
2.7 oz	85 mL	condensed cream of broccoli soup
3 oz	85 g	mild cheddar cheese
2¾ oz	78 g	scalloped potatoes mix
6 oz	170 g	smoked cooked ham

Check Your Shelves For:
golden seedless raisins
granulated sugar
mayonnaise
milk

P.S.
Stick a sheet of paper on your fridge to write down grocery items as you run out of them.

LOVE ISN'T GAZING INTO EACH OTHER'S
EYES, IT'S FOCUSING YOUR GAZE IN THE
SAME DIRECTION.

COOKING IT UP

FRIDAY - WEEK 1   10 minutes cooking time

SALMON SCRAMBLE

An easy-to-make meal that looks good and tastes the same.

4	4	large eggs
1 tbsp	15 mL	cold water
dash	dash	salt
dash	dash	pepper
3¾ oz	106 g	canned red sockeye salmon, drained and broken into small pieces
¼ tsp	1.2 mL	dry mustard
2 tbsp	30 mL	chopped green onion
2 tbsp	30 mL	chopped red pepper
1 tbsp	15 mL	vegetable oil

- Prepare Sour Cream Sauce (next page).
- In a small mixing bowl, fork-beat eggs, water, salt and pepper just until mixed.
- Stir in salmon, mustard, green onion and red pepper and mix well.
- Pour oil into a large frying pan, tilting to coat bottom and sides; heat 1 minute over medium/high heat or until oil is hot.
- Pour egg mixture into frying pan and reduce heat to medium.
- As mixture begins to set around the edges, stir with spatula to allow uncooked portion to run underneath.
- Cook 3 minutes or until egg mixture is set but still moist.
- Top with Sour Cream Sauce and serve.

Complete this meal with **Honeydew Melon Slices** and **Buttered Toast** on the side.

P.S.
An easy way to drain a tin (if you don't plan to save the juice) is to open it halfway and turn it on its side in the sink. After it has drained sufficiently, you can open it the rest of the way.

To slow the tears when chopping onion, place in the freezer 5 minutes just before cutting.

28

SOUR CREAM SAUCE

⅓ cup	**85 mL**	**sour cream**
⅓ cup	**85 mL**	**grated mild cheddar cheese**

- In a small saucepan, over medium/low heat, combine sour cream and cheese.
- Cook, stirring frequently, for 6 minutes or until cheese is melted.
- Remove from heat; cover to keep warm until ready to serve.

P.S.
Do not overcook the sauce, as prolonged cooking could cause the cheese to curdle.

GOING SHOPPING

3¾ oz	106 g	canned red sockeye salmon
4	4	eggs (large)
⅔ oz	18 g	green onion
½	½	honeydew melon (small)
1 oz	28 g	mild cheddar cheese
1 oz	28 g	red pepper
2.7 oz	85 mL	sour cream

Check Your Shelves For:
bread
butter or margarine
dry mustard
pepper
salt
vegetable oil

COOKING IT UP

No cooking time

Plan a picnic for a sunny day or, if it's raining or snowing, have an indoor picnic! Toss a blanket on the floor, add some festive music and spread out your picnic meal.

GARDEN SALAD (pictured on page 17)

1 cup	250 mL	broccoli flowerets
1 cup	250 mL	cauliflower flowerets
4	4	cherry tomatoes
2	2	green onions, quartered
4	4	very small mushrooms
¼ cup	60 mL	zesty Italian dressing

· In a small mixing bowl, combine all ingredients and refrigerate until required.

HOBOS (pictured on page 17)

1	1	mini French loaf
(to taste)		butter or margarine
(to taste)		Dijon mustard
2	2	lettuce leaves
8 oz	227 g	old fashioned ham slices
2	2	baby dill pickles, sliced
3	3	olives

· Slice French loaf in half lengthwise and spread with butter or margarine and mustard.
· Layer with lettuce, ham and pickles.
· To serve, cut diagonally in thirds and top with olives held in place with toothpicks.

P.S.
Store salads, dressings, etc. in refrigerator until required, cover with plastic wrap to prevent other fridge odors from penetrating.

ANTS ON A LOG (pictured on page 17)

No picnic would be complete without ants. Create your own with this recipe.

1	**1**	**celery stick, quartered**
2 oz	**57 g**	**process cheese spread**
24	**24**	**seedless raisins**

• Spread the celery with cheese, press on raisins and serve.

Clusters of **Seedless Green Grapes**, **Watermelon**, and **Sparkling Fruit Drinks** go well with this meal.

GOING SHOPPING

3 oz	85 g	broccoli flowerets
4 oz	114 g	cauliflower flowerets
1	1	celery stick
4	4	cherry tomatoes
1	1	French bread (mini loaf)
2	2	green onions
2	2	lettuce leaves
4	4	mushrooms (very small)
8 oz	227 g	old fashioned ham slices
2 oz	57 g	process cheese spread
5½ oz	156 g	seedless green grapes
2	2	sparkling fruit drinks
2 lbs	908 g	watermelon

Check Your Shelves For:
baby dill pickles
butter or margarine
Dijon mustard
olives
seedless raisins
zesty Italian dressing

COOKING IT UP

Time for a romantic evening? This meal makes an attractive dinner by candlelight.

TURKEY ROLL-UPS

5	5	thin frozen asparagus spears
1 cup	250 mL	boiling water
5	5	slices pre-cooked turkey breast
1 cup	250 mL	grated mozzarella cheese

- Preheat oven to 375°F (190°C).
- Rinse asparagus spears with boiling water; drain well.
- Place an asparagus spear on each slice of turkey; gently roll up and place seam side down in a medium casserole.
- Pour on sauce (below) and top with cheese.
- Cover and cook 30 minutes or until asparagus is fork-tender.

Serve with **Nectarine Wedges** as a side garnish.

P.S.
If only large size asparagus is available, cut in half and use only half for each turkey slice.

SAUCE

2 tsp	10 mL	butter or margarine
2 tsp	10 mL	corn starch
pinch	pinch	basil
½ tsp	2.5 mL	freeze-dried chives
½ cup	125 mL	milk

- In a small saucepan, over medium heat, melt butter or margarine.
- Combine remaining ingredients and add to melted butter or margarine.
- Cook and stir for 2 minutes or until sauce begins to thicken.

P.S.
To easily combine liquids and dry ingredients, put together in a small jar with a tight-fitting lid and shake vigorously.

ACORN SQUASH

1	1	medium acorn squash
1 tsp	5 mL	salt
2 cups	500 mL	hot water (approximately)
2 tsp	10 mL	butter or margarine
2 tsp	10 mL	brown sugar

- Wash squash, slice in half lengthwise and remove seeds.
- In a large saucepan, over high heat, bring salted water to a boil.
- Add squash, pulp side down, and return to a boil.
- Reduce heat to medium, cover and continue cooking 25 minutes or until pulp is tender; drain.
- Fluff pulp with a fork, dot with butter or margarine and sprinkle with brown sugar.
- Serve at once.

P.S.
If water appears to be boiling away, add a little more.

GOING SHOPPING

1 lb	454 g	acorn squash
6 oz	170 g	frozen asparagus spears
4 oz	114 g	mozzarella cheese
1	1	nectarine
10 oz	284 g	*pre-cooked sliced turkey breast

Check Your Shelves For:

basil	freeze-dried chives
brown sugar	milk
butter or margarine	salt
corn starch	

---

* *This is the deli-type turkey breast.*

NOTES

VEGETARIAN DAY

VEGETARIAN QUICHE, page 38
SPINACH SALAD, page 39

LOOKING IT OVER

WEEK 2

MONDAY
Vegetarian Quiche
Spinach Salad

TUESDAY
Roast Ribbons
Vermicelli

WEDNESDAY
Mexican Chicken

THURSDAY
Burger Barbecue
Pickles
Chips and Dip

FRIDAY
Tasty Tuna
Tomato Wedges

SATURDAY
Stuffed Croissants
Fruit 'n Dip

SUNDAY
Small Sausages
Apple Pancakes
Tangy Sauce

COOKING IT UP

This meal is so delicious, you'll want to lick the dishes when you're done.

VEGETARIAN QUICHE (pictured on page 35)

1 cup	250 mL	cauliflower flowerets
1 cup	250 mL	hot water
2	2	large eggs
1 cup	250 mL	light cream
¼ tsp	1.2 mL	salt
1 tsp	5 mL	baking powder
½ tsp	2.5 mL	dehydrated minced onion
¼ cup	60 mL	cake and pastry flour
½ cup	125 mL	grated Swiss cheese

- Preheat oven to 375°F (190°C).
- In a small covered saucepan, over medium heat, cook cauliflower in water for 10 minutes or until tender crisp; drain and chop.

- In a small mixing bowl, with mixer at medium speed, beat eggs until frothy.
- Add cream, salt, baking powder, onion and flour, while continuing to beat until well mixed.
- Stir in cheese and cooked cauliflower.
- Pour into 2 small well-greased quiche dishes.
- Bake 30 - 40 minutes or until top is tinged with gold and knife inserted near the centre comes out clean.
- Cool 5 minutes; serve in the quiche dishes.

P.S.
Add ½ tsp (2.5 mL) of raw rice to a salt shaker to keep the salt from becoming moist.

YOU CAN TELL THE HONEYMOON IS OVER
WHEN HE CALLS TO TELL HER THAT HE'LL
BE LATE FOR SUPPER AND SHE'S LEFT
HIM A NOTE SAYING IT'S IN THE FRIDGE.

SPINACH SALAD (pictured on page 35)

3 oz	85 g	small spinach leaves
1	1	small tomato, chopped
4	4	small mushrooms, sliced
2 oz	57 g	bean sprouts
¼ cup	60 mL	creamy salad dressing of your choice
2 tbsp	30 mL	flaked almonds

- Combine spinach, tomato, mushrooms and sprouts in 2 small salad bowls; cover with plastic wrap and refrigerate to keep crisp until required.
- Top with dressing and sprinkle with flaked almonds just before serving.

GOING SHOPPING

2 oz	57 g	bean sprouts
4 oz	114 g	cauliflower flowerets
2	2	eggs (large)
8 oz	250 mL	light cream
4	4	mushrooms (small)
3 oz	85 g	spinach leaves (small)
1½ oz	42 g	Swiss cheese
1	1	tomato (small)

Check Your Shelves For:
baking powder
cake and pastry flour
creamy salad dressing
dehydrated minced onion
flaked almonds
salt

P.S.
Write your grocery list on colored paper to make it easier to locate in your wallet or purse when shopping.

COOKING IT UP

ROAST RIBBONS

2 tbsp	30 mL	butter or margarine
2 tbsp	30 mL	all purpose flour
¼ oz	5 g	instant beef bouillon
¾ cup	185 mL	hot water
¼ cup	60 mL	spaghetti sauce
5 oz	142 g	cooked roast beef, cut into thin strips
½ cup	125 mL	sliced green pepper
½ cup	125 mL	onion wedges
1	1	medium tomato, cut into wedges

- In a medium saucepan, over medium heat, melt butter or margarine.
- Add flour; cook and stir for 2 minutes or until lightly browned.
- Dissolve beef bouillon in hot water and slowly add to flour mixture, stirring until smooth.
- Add remaining ingredients, reduce heat to medium/low and continue cooking, stirring frequently, for 7 minutes or until vegetables are tender and meat is well heated.
- Serve over pasta.

P.S.
This meal can be easily varied by serving Roast Ribbons over cooked rice instead of Pasta.

VERMICELLI

2 tsp	10 mL	salt
1½ qts	1½ L	hot water
6 oz	170 g	vermicelli
1 tbsp	15 mL	butter or margarine

- In a large saucepan, over medium/high heat, bring salted water to a boil.
- Break vermicelli in half for easier handling and stir into water.
- Reduce heat to medium and cook, stirring frequently, for 5 - 7 minutes or until tender; drain.
- Stir in butter or margarine and serve.

```
                        GOING SHOPPING

5 oz       142 g        *cooked roast beef (unsliced)
4 oz       114 g        green pepper
4 oz       114 g        onion
1          1            tomato (medium)


Check Your Shelves For:
all purpose flour
butter or margarine
instant beef bouillon
salt
spaghetti sauce
vermicelli
```

* We suggest pot roast or deli beef that will not toughen while cooking in liquids.

P.S.
Always check "best before" dates when buying dairy products, etc.

DID YOU KNOW?

Traditionally, in North America, buddies of an engaged young man throw a bachelor party for him before his marriage. This may have originated in old Greece. In that culture, before a man was married, he was given a final shave while friends gathered around to sing a farewell to his single days.

COOKING IT UP

15 minutes cooking time

The saying is "Acapulco is for lovers". If you can't fly there for dinner, you can create a Mexican atmosphere with these tasty dishes. Add a sombrero and maracas for extra fun.

MEXICAN CHICKEN

1½ cups	375 mL	shredded lettuce
1	1	medium tomato, chopped
2 tbsp	30 mL	chopped red pepper
½ cup	125 mL	grated mild cheddar cheese
24	24	taco flavored tortilla chips
¼ cup	60 mL	butter or margarine
5 tsp	25 mL	taco seasoning mix
1½ cups	375 mL	chopped cooked chicken
3 tbsp	45 mL	thick and chunky salsa
2 tbsp	30 mL	sour cream

- Layer lettuce, tomato, red pepper and then cheese on 2 dinner plates and line sides of plates with tortilla chips.
- In a small saucepan, over medium heat, combine butter or margarine, taco seasoning mix and chicken.
- Cook, stirring frequently, for 10 minutes or until chicken is well heated.
- Spoon over lettuce mixture.
- Spoon salsa and then sour cream onto middle of salad and serve.

A sumptuous dessert to finish off this meal, is **Almond Ice Cream**, see Sweet Things, page 93. When choosing this dessert, remember to include the required ingredients on your **Going Shopping** List.

P.S.
To easily shred lettuce, roll leaves lengthwise and thinly slice.

If your butter or margarine is hard, use the displacement method to measure it. For ¼ c (60 mL), fill a measuring cup ¾ full of cold water and add butter or margarine until the water reaches 1 cup (250 mL) level; drain.

GOING SHOPPING

6 oz	170 g	*cooked chicken
3 oz	85 g	lettuce leaves
1½ oz	42 g	mild cheddar cheese
1 oz	28 g	red pepper
1 oz	30 mL	sour cream
1	1	tomato (medium)
(optional)		sombrero, maracas

Check Your Shelves For:
butter or margarine
taco flavored tortilla chips
taco seasoning mix
thick and chunky salsa

See Monday - Week 1, page 20 or order from the Deli. (Dark meat or a blend of dark and white meat works best in the Mexican Chicken recipe.)

P.S.
To store fresh vegetables: wash, drain, pat dry and refrigerate as soon as you return from the store. Keep lettuce in a large ventilated plastic bag as leaves turn brown when tightly packed or covered.

TO KEEP YOUR MARRIAGE GLOWING
CAN TAKE JUST A SENTENCE OR TWO;
"YOU MAY BE RIGHT"
OR
"I LOVE YOU"

COOKING IT UP

You can enjoy this great western style meal year-round. When the weather turns too cold to barbecue, just pop the burgers under the broiler.

<u>BURGER BARBECUE</u>

½ lb	227 g	lean ground beef
1	1	large egg
¼ cup	60 mL	crushed bacon crackers
3 tbsp	45 mL	onion soup mix
(optional)		barbecue sauce
2 or 3	2 or 3	hamburger buns
(optional)		tomato slices
(optional)		lettuce leaves

- Preheat barbecue (or broiler, in off-season, if manufacturer directs).
- In a medium mixing bowl, combine ground beef, egg, crackers and soup mix.
- Shape into 2 or 3 patties and spread with barbecue sauce (if desired).
- Barbecue (or broil with broiling pan 3" (8 cm) from source of heat) for 4 minutes, each side, or until meat is **well-cooked**.
- Toast hamburger buns on barbecue (or under broiler) for 10 - 15 seconds.
- Put hamburger patties on buns and (if desired) garnish with tomato slices and lettuce leaves.
- Serve at once.

To complement this meal, serve with **Pickles**, **Potato Chips** and **Chip Dip**.

P.S.
To easily crush chips or crackers, place in a plastic bag (being careful not to trap a lot of air), secure with a twist tie, and roll with a rolling pin.

THE BETTER SHE LOOKS,
THE LONGER HE DOES.

GOING SHOPPING

1 oz	28 g	chip dip
1	1	egg (large)
2 or 3	2 or 3	hamburger buns
½ lb	227 g	lean ground beef
(optional)		lettuce
(optional)		tomato (medium)

Check Your Shelves For:
bacon crackers
barbecue sauce (optional)
onion soup mix
pickles
regular potato chips

DID YOU KNOW?

In North America, a ring is often given as a mutual pledge of engagement. In the 18th century, in some countries, the custom was quite different. Young women, wishing to be married, walked throughout the town without any covering on their heads. If a bachelor saw one he desired to make his bride, he would throw an embroidered handkerchief or some other article of his clothing over her head. The young woman would then consider herself engaged and stay within the confines of her home until the day of the wedding.

COOKING IT UP

TASTY TUNA

Many people like eating fish on Fridays, but this recipe is so tasty you'll want to serve it on more occasions than that.

½ tsp	2.5 mL	salt
1 qt	1 L	hot water
⅓ cup	85 mL	macaroni
6½ oz	184 g	canned flaked light tuna, drained
10 oz	284 mL	condensed cream of mushroom soup
2 tbsp	30 mL	diced dill pickle
3 tbsp	45 mL	chopped green onion
¾ cup	185 mL	crushed regular potato chips
¾ cup	185 mL	grated mild cheddar cheese

- Preheat oven to 400°F (200°C).
- In a medium saucepan, over medium/high heat, bring salted water to a boil.
- Stir in macaroni and cook, stirring occasionally, for 6 minutes or until tender; drain.

- In a small well-greased casserole, combine cooked macaroni with tuna, soup, pickle, green onion and ½ cup (125 mL) potato chips; cover and bake 10 minutes.
- Sprinkle with remaining chips and grated cheese; cover and bake 15 more minutes or until hot and bubbly.
- Remove from oven and serve.

P.S.
To safely dispose of a tin lid, carefully put it inside the empty can before placing it in the trash.

DUTY MAKES US DO THINGS WELL, BUT
LOVE MAKES US DO THEM CHEERFULLY.

TOMATO WEDGES

So simple, yet colorful - makes an attractive addition to any meal!

1	1	medium tomato
2	2	lettuce leaves
2 tbsp	30 mL	creamy salad dressing of your choice

- Cut the tomato into wedges.
- Place on lettuce leaves and top with salad dressing.
- Serve as a side salad.

GOING SHOPPING

6½ oz	184 g	canned flaked light tuna
10 oz	284 mL	condensed cream of mushroom soup
1 oz	28 g	green onion
2	2	lettuce leaves
2¼ oz	64 g	mild cheddar cheese
1	1	tomato (medium)

Check Your Shelves For:
creamy salad dressing
dill pickles
macaroni
regular potato chips
salt

P.S.
To save time, shop early in the day or during the middle of the week when the stores are less crowded.

COOKING IT UP

SATURDAY - WEEK 2   15 minutes cooking time

Set out your good china - this fabulous meal will even impress your Mother-in-Law! (Since this meal is designed for 2, remember to increase your recipe ingredients and Going Shopping amounts when you invite company.)

STUFFED CROISSANTS

2	2	large fresh croissants
4 oz	114 g	thinly sliced cooked ham
4 oz	114 g	cooked chicken, sliced
2	2	large mushrooms, sliced
1½ tbsp	22.5 mL	chopped green onion
½ cup	125 mL	grated mild cheddar cheese

- Preheat oven to 425°F (215°C).
- Slice croissants in half and put bottom halves on a pizza pan.
- Layer with ham, chicken, mushrooms, and then green onion.
- Spoon on sauce (below); bake 5 minutes.
- Sprinkle with cheese and bake 5 more minutes or until well heated (during the last minute of baking, cover with top croissant halves).
- Remove from oven and serve.

WHITE SAUCE

1½ tbsp	22.5 mL	butter or margarine
1½ tbsp	22.5 mL	all purpose flour
½ cup	125 mL	milk

- In a small saucepan, over medium heat, melt butter or margarine.
- Combine flour and milk and slowly add to melted butter or margarine.
- Cook, while stirring, for 2 minutes or until sauce thickens.

P.S.
Grated cheese keeps well in the refrigerator or freezer. Date and store in a plastic bag.

LOVE RESEMBLES A COLD: EASILY
CAUGHT - DIFFICULT TO REMEDY.

FRUIT 'N DIP

½	½	small cantaloupe
1	1	kiwi, peeled and sliced
¼ cup	60 mL	red seedless grapes
1	1	small banana, peeled and sliced
6 oz	170 g	peach yogurt
3 tbsp	45 mL	icing or confectioners' sugar

- Scoop balls of cantaloupe with a melon scoop.
- Mix fruit and put into 2 ramekins.
- Combine yogurt with icing or confectioners' sugar and serve in 2 small bowls as a dip for fruit.

GOING SHOPPING

1	1	banana (small)
½	½	cantaloupe (small)
4 oz	114 g	*cooked chicken
4 oz	114 g	cooked ham (thinly sliced)
2	2	fresh croissants (large)
½ oz	14 g	green onion
1	1	kiwi
1½ oz	42 g	mild cheddar cheese
2	2	mushrooms (large)
6 oz	170 g	peach yogurt
2 oz	57 g	red seedless grapes

Check Your Shelves For:
all purpose flour
butter or margarine
icing or confectioners' sugar
milk

Refer to Monday - Week 1, page 20 or order from Deli.

COOKING IT UP

Pancakes and Sausages for breakfast - what a yummy way to start the day.

SMALL SAUSAGES

8   8   **breakfast sausages**

- Preheat oven to 400°F (200°C).
- Place sausages in a small casserole and bake, turning once, for 20 minutes or until meat loses its pink color inside.
- Drain and serve.

P.S.
Never pour grease down your drain (it could clog it). Instead, drain into a cup and when set, scoop into a plastic bag for trash collection.

APPLE PANCAKES

This pancake recipe has an unusual twist - a wonderful apple taste.

1 cup	250 mL	**regular pancake mix**
½ cup	125 mL	**milk**
½ cup	125 mL	**apple juice**
1	1	**large egg**
1 tbsp	15 mL	**vegetable oil**
(to taste)		**butter or margarine**

- In a small mixing bowl, combine pancake mix, milk, apple juice, egg and oil; beat until smooth.
- Pour batter by ¼ cups (60 mL) into hot, lightly greased, large frying pan.
- Cook over medium heat for 1 - 2 minutes or until bottom of pancake is golden brown; turn and cook remaining side.
- To serve, dot with butter or margarine and top with Tangy Sauce (next page).

TANGY SAUCE

1 tbsp	15 mL	cornstarch
½ tsp	2.5 mL	ground cinnamon
⅓ cup	85 mL	apple juice
⅓ cup	85 mL	crabapple jelly

- In a small saucepan, blend cornstarch, cinnamon and apple juice; add crabapple jelly.
- Cook over medium heat, stirring frequently, for 5 minutes or until sauce thickens slightly and jelly is blended in.
- Remove from heat, cover and keep warm until ready to serve.

SOME PEOPLE SAY MARRIAGES ARE MADE IN
HEAVEN, BUT THEN ISN'T STORMY WEATHER?

GOING SHOPPING

6.5 oz	210 mL	apple juice
9 oz	255 g	breakfast sausages
1	1	egg (large)

Check Your Shelves For:
butter or margarine
cornstarch
crabapple jelly
ground cinnamon
milk
regular pancake mix
vegetable oil

NOTES

ROMANTIC MOVIE NIGHT

PIZZA, page 58
ICED POPCORN, page 58

LOOKING IT OVER

WEEK 3

MONDAY
Chicken Wings
Vegetable Rice

TUESDAY
Pizza
Iced Popcorn

WEDNESDAY
Creamy Broccoli Soup
Cheese Rolls

THURSDAY
Chuckwagon Dinner
Buttermilk Biscuits

FRIDAY
Crab Melt
Spiral Pasta
Peach Slices

SATURDAY
French Toast
Bacon
Green Grapes on the Vine

SUNDAY
Chinese Chicken
Mandarin Fruit Salad
Chinese Tea

COOKING IT UP

CHICKEN WINGS

It's worth breaking a diet over this one!

| 1¼ lb | 568 g | chicken wings |
| ¼ tsp | 1.2 mL | salt |

- Preheat oven to 350°F (180°C)
- Cut off wing tips (discard or save for soup base); sever remaining wings at joint.
- Place on foil lined cookie sheet, sprinkle with salt and bake 20 minutes.
- Brush with half the Sweet & Sour Sauce (below) and continue baking 20 more minutes.
- Turn wings, brush with remaining sauce and bake 10 more minutes or until chicken is tender.
- Remove from oven and serve.

SWEET & SOUR SAUCE

½ cup	125 mL	packed brown sugar
4 tsp	20 mL	all purpose flour
1 tbsp	15 mL	ketchup
2 tbsp	30 mL	red wine vinegar
4 tsp	20 mL	soy sauce
2 tbsp	30 mL	water

- In a small saucepan, over medium heat, blend all ingredients.
- Stir and cook 3 minutes or until mixture boils and thickens; remove from heat.

A nice addition to this meal is warm **Dinner Rolls**.

P.S.
To soften hardened brown sugar, put a slice of soft bread in the package; close tightly and leave for a day.

VEGETABLE RICE

A colorful change from the usual rice - and so tasty too!

½ cup	125 mL	natural long grain rice
1 tbsp	15 mL	butter or margarine
½ tsp	2.5 mL	salt
1 cup	250 mL	frozen small mixed vegetables
1¼ cups	310 mL	boiling water

- Preheat oven to 350°F (180°C).
- In a small greased casserole, combine all ingredients except water.
- Stir in **boiling** water.
- Cover and bake 35 - 40 minutes or just until liquid is absorbed (do not overcook).
- Fluff with a fork and serve.

P.S.
It is very important to have the water boiling when you stir it in - if you let it cool, the recipe will not work.

GOING SHOPPING

1¼ lb	568 g	chicken wings
2	2	dinner rolls
5 oz	142 g	frozen small mixed vegetables

Check Your Shelves For:
all purpose flour
brown sugar
butter or margarine
ketchup
natural long grain rice
red wine vinegar
salt
soy sauce

COOKING IT UP

What better way to spend an evening than with Pizza, Popcorn and a Romantic Movie (you can rent a video and VCR if you don't own one). Begin this meal by making the Iced Popcorn and while it's cooling, bake the Pizza.

PIZZA (pictured on page 53)

½ cup	125 mL	pizza sauce
12"	30 cm	pizza crust
2¼ cups	560 mL	grated mozzarella cheese
2 oz	57 g	pizza pepperoni slices
1	1	small green pepper, sliced
2	2	large mushrooms, sliced
1	1	small tomato, chopped
½ cup	125 mL	sliced onion
¼ cup	60 mL	sliced black olives

- Place pizza pan in oven and preheat to 475°F (245°C).
- Spread pizza sauce on pizza crust and sprinkle evenly with cheese.
- Layer remaining ingredients on crust.
- Place pizza on hot pan and bake 10 - 12 minutes or until the bottom is brown and cheese is bubbling throughout.
- Remove from oven and let cool slightly.
- Slice and serve.

As you enjoy your pizza, treat yourself to a cool **Cherry Pop**.

ICED POPCORN (pictured on page 53)

With the cherry taste and pretty red color - this is no ordinary popcorn!

¼ cup	60 mL	popping corn, popped
¼ cup	60 mL	butter or margarine
½ cup	125 mL	icing or confectioners' sugar
2 tbsp	30 mL	corn syrup
¼ tsp	1.2 mL	salt
⅛ tsp	.6 mL	baking soda
¼ tsp	1.2 mL	cherry extract
¼ tsp	1.2 mL	red food coloring

(continued on next page)

- Preheat oven to 200°F (100°C).
- Put popped popcorn in a large mixing bowl.
- In a small saucepan, over medium heat, combine butter or margarine, icing or confectioners' sugar, syrup and salt.
- Heat, stirring frequently, until mixture comes to a boil, then boil 5 minutes without stirring.
- Remove from heat and stir in remaining ingredients; pour over popcorn and mix until well coated.
- Spread over cookie sheet and bake 15 minutes to dry.
- Cool, stirring occasionally, for 15 minutes and serve.

P.S.
This recipe can be made ahead and stored for several days in a plastic bag or frozen until needed. It can easily be doubled if more iced popcorn is desired.

GOING SHOPPING

1	1	green pepper (small)
6¾ oz	191 g	mozzarella cheese
2	2	mushrooms (large)
4 oz	114 g	onion
12"	30 cm	pizza crust
2 oz	57 g	pizza pepperoni slices
4 oz	125 mL	pizza sauce
2 oz	57 g	popping corn
2	2	tins cherry pop
1	1	tomato (small)
1	1	romantic movie video

Check Your Shelves For:
baking soda
butter or margarine
cherry extract
corn syrup

icing or confectioners' sugar
red food coloring
salt
sliced black olives

COOKING IT UP

WEDNESDAY - WEEK 3

40 minutes cooking time

What could be more inviting then a hot cup of soup? This is great any time - after work, a late night snack - or increase the ingredients and invite the gang.

CREAMY BROCCOLI SOUP

¼ cup	60 mL	minced onion
1 tbsp	15 mL	butter or margarine
10 oz	284 mL	condensed chicken broth soup
4 oz	114 g	frozen chopped broccoli
½ cup	125 mL	grated potato
pinch	pinch	tarragon
1 tbsp	15 mL	all purpose flour
1 cup	250 mL	light cream

- In a small saucepan, over medium heat, saute onion in butter or margarine, stirring frequently, for 2 minutes.
- Add chicken broth, broccoli, potato and tarragon; bring to a boil.
- Cover and cook, stirring occasionally, for 20 minutes or until broccoli and potato are tender; mash vegetables.
- Combine flour and cream and add to soup mixture.
- Reduce heat to medium/low and, stirring frequently, cook uncovered (do not boil) for 10 more minutes.
- Serve warm.

P.S.
Store onions in a cool, dry, well ventilated place.

THERE ARE TWO GOOD BOOKS THAT
CAN BE HELPFUL IN A MARRIAGE:

"COOKBOOK" AND "CHECKBOOK"

CHEESE ROLLS

8¼ oz	235 g	crescent rolls
½ cup	125 mL	grated mild cheddar cheese
3 tbsp	45 mL	finely chopped onion
(to taste)		butter or margarine

- Preheat oven to 425°F (220°C).
- Spread each crescent roll with cheese and onion and roll up, beginning at largest end.
- Place, not touching, on a cookie sheet and bake 12 minutes or until golden.
- Serve warm with butter or margarine.

P.S.
Leftover rolls can be reheated for a snack the following day.

GOING SHOPPING

10 oz	284 mL	condensed chicken broth soup
8¼ oz	235 g	crescent rolls
4 oz	114 g	frozen chopped broccoli
8 oz	250 mL	light cream
1½ oz	42 g	mild cheddar cheese
2 oz	57 g	onion
1	1	potato (medium)

Check Your Shelves For:
all purpose flour
butter or margarine
tarragon

P.S.
Become familiar with the store you shop at and group the grocery items on your list according to the store layout - meats, dairy products, etc. This will save you time when shopping.

COOKING IT UP

CHUCKWAGON DINNER

Meat and vegetables in this casserole makes it a meal in itself.

8 oz	225 g	extra lean ground beef
¼ cup	60 mL	chopped onion
9 oz	256 mL	canned whole white potatoes, well drained
¼ oz	5 g	instant beef bouillon
1 tsp	5 mL	corn starch
½ tsp	2.5 mL	prepared mustard
pinch	pinch	garlic powder
7 oz	198 mL	canned stewed tomatoes
½ cup	125 mL	frozen small mixed vegetables

- Preheat oven to 425°F (220°C).
- In a small frying pan, over medium/high heat, cook ground beef and onion, stirring frequently, for 7 minutes or until meat loses its pink color.
- Remove from heat and drain.
- Cut smaller potatoes into 4 pieces and larger ones into 8.
- In a small casserole, combine all ingredients.
- Cover and bake 30 minutes or until vegetables are fork-tender and well heated.
- Serve hot.

A tasty companion for this meal is **Buttermilk Biscuits**.

P.S.
Leftover potatoes and stewed tomatoes may be frozen and stored for future casseroles or used in soups.

After working with raw meats or poultry, wash all utensils, cutting boards, hands, etc. in hot soapy water to avoid spreading bacteria found in raw meats and poultry.

MARRIAGE IS THE RADIANCE OF LOVE.

GOING SHOPPING

4	4	buttermilk biscuits (small)
7 oz	198 mL	canned stewed tomatoes
9 oz	256 mL	canned whole white potatoes
8 oz	225 g	extra lean ground beef
3½ oz	100 g	frozen small mixed vegetables
2 oz	57 g	onion

Check Your Shelves For:
corn starch
garlic powder
instant beef bouillon
prepared mustard

P.S.
Meats such as ground beef, stewing beef, etc. should be stored in the fridge only 1 - 2 days.

DID YOU KNOW?

Here in North America, the wedding ring is an integral part of the marriage ceremony - it was popular in prehistoric times too. In that day, a man tied a rope of grass around his waist and one around his mate's waist, wrist and ankle to show their permanent attachment to each other. In early Roman times, a bridegroom sent an iron ring to his betrothed to demonstrate how enduring their union should be. Today's wedding bands are usually made of gold, but they still symbolize a lasting relationship.

COOKING IT UP

Start this meal by preparing the Pasta and then while it's cooking, make the Crab Melt.

CRAB MELT

4 tsp	20 mL	butter or margarine
4 tsp	20 mL	all purpose flour
¾ cup	185 mL	milk
½ cup	125 mL	grated mild cheddar cheese
1	1	egg yolk
1 tsp	5 mL	prepared mustard
2 tbsp	30 mL	chopped green onion
2 tbsp	30 mL	chopped red pepper
4 oz	114 g	snow crab

- In a medium saucepan, over medium heat, melt butter or margarine.
- Combine flour and milk and add to melted butter or margarine; stir in cheese.
- Cook and stir for 2 minutes or until cheese is melted and sauce begins to thicken.
- Reduce heat to low, add remaining ingredients and cook, stirring frequently to prevent sticking, for 5 more minutes.
- Spoon over pasta and serve.

Peach Slices add a tangy touch to this meal; serve them as a side garnish.

P.S.
Fresh, frozen, or canned snow crab is acceptable for this recipe. Frozen snow crab must be thawed, and canned crab must be drained before use.

Leftover egg white can be frozen for up to two months and used to make a Torte, see Something Special - Christmas, page 124.

WHEN YOU QUESTION YOUR SPOUSE'S
JUDGEMENT, REMEMBER WHO CHOSE YOU.

SPIRAL PASTA

More showy than spaghetti or macaroni, but just as easy to make.

1 tsp	5 mL	salt
1½ qts	1½ L	hot water
1½ cups	375 mL	small spiral pasta
1 tbsp	15 mL	butter or margarine

- In a large saucepan, over medium/high heat, bring salted water to a boil.
- Add pasta and boil, stirring occasionally, for 10 - 15 minutes or until tender; drain.
- Toss with butter or margarine before serving.

KEEP YOUR EYES WIDE OPEN BEFORE
YOU WED AND HALF CLOSED AFTER.

GOING SHOPPING

1	1	egg (large)
⅔ oz	18 g	green onion
1½ oz	42 g	mild cheddar cheese
1	1	peach
1 oz	28 g	red pepper
4 oz	114 g	snow crab
7 oz	198 g	spiral pasta (small)

Check Your Shelves For:
all purpose flour
butter or margarine
milk
prepared mustard
salt

COOKING IT UP

Whether you serve this meal for breakfast, lunch or dinner, you can't go wrong. It's pleasing to the eye with a taste that's hard to beat.

ORANGE SAUCE

A versatile sauce - great over French Toast and pancakes too.

1 tbsp	15 mL	cornstarch
pinch	pinch	orange peel spice
½ cup	125 mL	orange juice
1 tbsp	15 mL	orange marmalade

- In a small saucepan, combine all ingredients.
- Cook over medium heat, stirring occasionally, for 3 minutes or until sauce thickens.
- Remove from heat and cover to keep warm until required.

FRENCH TOAST

2	2	large eggs
5 tbsp	75 mL	orange juice
¼ tsp	1.2 mL	salt
¼ tsp	1.2 mL	vanilla
¼ cup	60 mL	vegetable oil
4	4	thick white bread slices, cut diagonally in halves
4 tsp	20 mL	pecan pieces

- Preheat oven to 400°F (200°C).
- In a medium mixing bowl, fork-beat eggs, orange juice, salt and vanilla until frothy.
- Pour oil onto a cookie sheet and tilt to coat bottom; place in oven and preheat 2 minutes.
- Meanwhile, dip bread in egg mixture to coat.
- Place in a single layer on cookie sheet.
- Bake each side for 5 minutes or until lightly browned.
- Top with Orange Sauce (above) and sprinkle with pecans.

Serve with **Green Grapes on the Vine** as a side garnish.

BACON

10	10	side bacon slices

- In a large frying pan, over medium heat, fry bacon, turning occasionally, for 10 minutes or according to taste.
- Lift bacon onto a paper towel to drain.
- Serve warm.

P.S.
Excess bacon may be fried, then crumbled and frozen for future use as a garnish.

THE TROUBLE IN MARRIAGE OFTEN
STARTS WHEN THE MAN IS SO BUSY
BRINGING HOME THE BACON THAT HE
FORGETS HIS SUGAR.

GOING SHOPPING

2	2	eggs (large)
4½ oz	128 g	seedless green grapes on the vine
10	10	side bacon slices
4	4	thick white bread slices

<u>Check Your Shelves For</u>:
corn starch
orange juice
orange marmalade
orange peel spice
pecan pieces
salt
vanilla
vegetable oil

COOKING IT UP

SUNDAY - WEEK 3

Set out some chopsticks and give this Chinese style meal a try!

CHINESE CHICKEN

10 oz	284 mL	condensed cream of mushroom soup
dash	dash	pepper
1½ cups	375 mL	chopped cooked chicken
4 oz	113 mL	canned water chestnuts, drained
¼ cup	60 mL	chopped onion
½ cup	125 mL	cashew nut pieces
1 cup	250 mL	chow mein noodles

- Preheat oven to 375°F (190°C).
- In a small casserole, combine all ingredients (saving some noodles for garnish) and mix well.
- Cover and bake 30 - 35 minutes or until hot and bubbly.
- During last 5 minutes of baking, remove cover and sprinkle with remaining noodles.
- Serve hot.

P.S.
Leftover water chestnuts may be frozen for future casserole use.

MANDARIN FRUIT SALAD

¼ cup	60 mL	whipped topping
1 tbsp	15 mL	mayonnaise
¼ tsp	1.2 mL	orange extract
10 oz	284 mL	canned mandarin orange segments, drained
2	2	butter lettuce leaves

- In a small mixing bowl, combine whipped topping, mayonnaise and orange extract; refrigerate until required.
- Just before serving, fold in orange segments and spoon onto crisp lettuce leaves.

This meal wouldn't be complete without **Chinese Tea**, be sure to include it.

GOING SHOPPING

2	2	butter lettuce leaves
10 oz	284 mL	canned mandarin orange segments
4 oz	113 mL	canned water chestnuts
10 oz	284 mL	condensed cream of mushroom soup
4½ oz	128 g	*cooked chicken
2 oz	57 g	onion
2 oz	60 mL	whipped topping

Check Your Shelves For:
**cashew nut pieces
Chinese tea
chow mein noodles
mayonnaise
orange extract
pepper

---

*   *Refer to Monday - Week 1, page 20 or you could use deli or canned chicken.*

** *You will need the type of cashews used for snacking, not the cooking variety, as the snacking type contain salt.*

TODAY WHEN NEWLYWEDS FEATHER THEIR
NEST, YOU'LL USUALLY FIND FOUR
PARENTS WHO HAVE BEEN PLUCKED.

NOTES

BREAKFAST IN BED

FRESH STRAWBERRIES, page 86
RAISIN TEA BISCUITS, page 86
DELICIOUS COFFEE, page 87

LOOKING IT OVER

WEEK 4

MONDAY
Bavarian Stew
Dumplings

TUESDAY
Wiener Wraps
Saucy Beans

WEDNESDAY
Little Loaves
Corn Cobs
Tomato Cups

THURSDAY
Planned Over Chili
Crusty Bun Bowls

FRIDAY
Shrimp Sandwiches
Fries

SATURDAY
Chicken Royale
Cabbage and Apple Mix

SUNDAY
Fresh Strawberries
Raisin Tea Biscuits
Delicious Coffee

COOKING IT UP

BAVARIAN STEW

This stew may be unlike those you are familiar with, because of its unique blend of ingredients, but you're sure to enjoy its European flavor. It can be served with or without dumplings.

8 oz	227 g	Polish sausage
10 oz	284 mL	condensed beef broth soup
¾ cup	185 mL	water
¾ cup	185 mL	bottled wine sauerkraut, drained
1	1	medium Golden Delicious apple, peeled, cored and cut into 8 pieces
pinch	pinch	celery seeds
3 tbsp	45 mL	golden seedless raisins
3 tbsp	45 mL	corn starch

- Peel casing from sausage and cut in 1" (2.5 cm) lengths.
- Put all ingredients in a medium saucepan and mix well.
- Spoon dumplings (next page) onto stew and cook over medium heat for 10 minutes; cover, reduce to low and continue cooking another 10 minutes.
- Serve hot.

P.S.
Extra sauerkraut can be stored in the refrigerator for future use.

Leftover sausage could be used in place of pepperoni slices on the pizza, see Tuesday - Week 3, page 58.

DON'T TRY TO FIND OUT
WHO'S BOSS - YOU'LL BOTH
BE HAPPIER NOT KNOWING.

DUMPLINGS

This fluffy alternative to dinner rolls gives an extra special touch to this meal.

½ cup	125 mL	all purpose flour
¼ tsp	1.2 mL	salt
¾ tsp	3.7 mL	baking powder
¼ cup	60 mL	milk
1 tbsp	15 mL	vegetable oil

- In a small mixing bowl, combine flour, salt and baking powder.
- Combine milk and oil and quickly stir into flour mixture until soft dough forms (do not over mix).
- Drop by heaping tablespoons onto Stew to cook.
- Serve with Stew.

P.S.
Dumplings are good in other stews as well.

GOING SHOPPING

6 oz	185 mL	bottled wine sauerkraut
10 oz	284 mL	condensed beef broth soup
1	1	Golden Delicious apple (medium)
8 oz	227 g	Polish sausage

Check Your Shelves For:
all purpose flour
baking powder
celery seeds
corn starch
golden seedless raisins
milk
salt
vegetable oil

COOKING IT UP

Hot Dogs and Beans - fast and easy, but with an unusual flair that separates them from the ordinary.

SAUCY BEANS

14 oz	398 mL	canned beans in tomato sauce
1 tbsp	15 mL	brown sugar
¼ tsp	1.2 mL	dry mustard
½ tsp	2.5 mL	dehydrated minced onion
1 tbsp	15 mL	ketchup
1 tsp	5 mL	worcestershire sauce

- In a small saucepan, over medium/low heat, combine all ingredients.
- Cook 20 minutes, stirring frequently to blend flavors.
- Cool slightly and serve.

WIENER WRAPS

4	4	turkey wieners
(optional)		mild cheddar cheese wedges
4	4	wiener wraps

- Preheat oven to 375°F (190°C).
- If desired, slice wieners halfway through lengthwise and insert cheddar cheese wedges.
- Roll wieners in wrap.
- Place on a pizza pan, making sure they don't touch, and bake 12 - 15 minutes or until wrap is golden brown and wieners are cooked through.
- Remove from oven and serve.

P.S.
Remaining wiener wrap can be sprinkled with a little brown sugar, cinnamon, raisins, and dotted with butter, then rolled and baked at 375°C (190°C) for 12 - 15 minutes or until golden brown.

GOING SHOPPING

14 oz	398 mL	canned beans in tomato sauce
(optional)		mild cheddar cheese
7 oz	198 g	package wiener wrap dough
4	4	turkey wieners

Check Your Shelves For:
brown sugar
dehydrated minced onion
dry mustard
ketchup
worcestershire sauce

P.S.
Extra wieners can be frozen for future use.

Grate ends or hard pieces of cheese and store in tightly covered jars. Use as a garnish or in recipes requiring grated cheese.

DID YOU KNOW?

After the ceremony in Old English marriages, the father of the bride would take her shoe off and hand it to the groom. By receiving it, the husband became her master. In later years, a shoe tied to the back of the couple's car was a symbol that the father was giving up his authority over his daughter. Today, cars are more likely to be decorated with flowers or balloons.

COOKING IT UP

LITTLE LOAVES

Meat loaf with a difference - veal that ranks with the best.

12 oz	341 g	ground veal
¼ cup	60 mL	bread crumbs
¼ oz	5 g	instant beef bouillon
1 tbsp	15 mL	dehydrated minced onion
½ tsp	2.5 mL	parsley flakes
¼ tsp	1.2 mL	salt
1	1	large egg
2 tbsp	30 mL	milk
(optional)		ketchup

- Preheat oven to 425°F (215°C).
- In a medium mixing bowl, thoroughly mix all ingredients, except ketchup.
- Shape into 4 loaves and place in a medium greased casserole.
- Bake 30 - 35 minutes or until meat loses its pink color inside.
- Serve warm with ketchup (if desired).

CORN COBS

A favorite of many!

1 tsp	5 mL	salt
2 qts	2 L	hot water
2	2	medium frozen corn cobs
(to taste)		butter or margarine

- In a large saucepan, over medium/high heat, bring salted water to a boil.
- Add corn and return to a boil.
- Cook 7 - 9 minutes or until kernels are fork-tender; drain.
- Serve with butter or margarine.

P.S.

In season, you may prefer to use fresh corn - cooking time may vary slightly.

TOMATO CUPS

These stuffed tomatoes are a fun addition to any meal.

2	2	ripe medium tomatoes
3 tbsp	45 mL	bread crumbs
2 tbsp	30 mL	mayonnaise
dash	dash	salt
dash	dash	pepper

- Cut tops off tomatoes; discard tops.
- Scoop out pulp, leaving a ¼" (6 mm) shell; invert tomatoes on paper towel to drain.
- In a small bowl, mash pulp with a fork; drain.
- Combine pulp with bread crumbs, mayonnaise, salt and pepper.
- Spoon tomato mixture into shells.
- Refrigerate until ready to serve.

P.S.
For something different, just before serving, top stuffed tomatoes with a little grated cheese and broil 1 minute or until cheese melts.

GOING SHOPPING

1	1	egg (large)
2	2	frozen corn cobs (medium)
12 oz	341 g	ground veal
2	2	ripe tomatoes (medium)

Check Your Shelves For:

bread crumbs	mayonnaise
butter or margarine	milk
dehydrated minced onion	parsley flakes
instant beef bouillon	pepper
ketchup (optional)	salt

COOKING IT UP

THURSDAY - WEEK 4

*You can quickly **thaw the meat sauce** for this popular meal in a microwave or allow approximately 24 hours thawing time in the refrigerator.*

PLANNED OVER CHILI

This savory dish is served in a unique way - in Crusty Bun Bowls .

		*meat sauce, thawed
7 oz	198 mL	canned pinto beans, drained
2 tsp	10 mL	chili powder
2 tbsp	30 mL	sour cream
2 tbsp	30 mL	grated mild cheddar cheese
1 tbsp	15 mL	chopped onion

- Preheat oven to 350°F (180°C).
- In a medium saucepan, mix thawed meat sauce, pinto beans and chili powder (extra chili powder can be added for a spicier taste).
- Cook over medium heat, stirring occasionally, for 10 minutes or until heated through.
- Spoon the chili into Crusty Bun Bowls (next page) - this may overflow - and top with sour cream, cheddar cheese and then onion.
- Serve hot.

For a cool refreshing drink to serve with this meal, try **Carbonated Water** with a slice of **Lime**.

* See Tuesday - Week 1, page 22.

P.S.
Chopped onion freezes well. You may want to chop a whole onion and store in a container for use in other recipes.

ARCHAEOLOGISTS MAKE BETTER
HUSBANDS - THE OLDER SHE GROWS,
THE MORE INTEREST HE SHOWS.

CRUSTY BUN BOWLS

2	2	extra large crusty buns

- Preheat oven to 350°F (180°C).
- Cut thin tops off buns.
- Scoop out some of the inside leaving a ½" (1.2 cm) shell.
- Place bun shells on a pizza pan and bake 5 minutes.
- Serve in place of a regular bowl for Chili or thick soups.

P.S.
Bread scooped out of buns could be fed to the birds or dried and crumbled for use in future recipes.

EVERY MAN NEEDS A WIFE...SOME
THINGS THAT GO WRONG JUST CAN'T
BE BLAMED ON THE GOVERNMENT.

GOING SHOPPING

7 oz	198 mL	canned pinto beans
12 oz	330 mL	carbonated water
2	2	crusty buns (extra large)
1	1	lime (small)
⅓ oz	9 g	mild cheddar cheese
½ oz	14 g	onion
1 oz	30 mL	sour cream

Check Your Shelves For:
chili powder
meat sauce

P.S.
For best food selection, check with your grocery store manager to see when they do their restocking.

COOKING IT UP

The British are known for their "fish and fries" wrapped in newspaper. Here's another seafood recipe that goes great with fries.

SHRIMP SANDWICHES

6 oz	170 g	small cooked shrimp
½ tsp	2.5 mL	lemon juice
2 tbsp	30 mL	finely chopped onion
2 tbsp	30 mL	finely chopped celery
3 tbsp	45 mL	mayonnaise
2 tsp	10 mL	creamy cucumber dressing and dip mix
4	4	fresh bread slices
(to taste)		butter or margarine
2	2	*lettuce leaves, crisp

- In a small mixing bowl, combine shrimp, lemon juice, onion, and celery; toss to mix.
- Chill a minimum of 10 minutes.
- Combine mayonnaise and cucumber dressing and add to chilled shrimp mixture; drain just before preparing sandwiches.
- Spread bread slices with butter or margarine.
- Put shrimp mixture on 2 slices of bread.
- Top with lettuce leaves and remaining slices of bread.
- Angle cut sandwiches and serve.

   * To crisp lettuce leaves, rinse with cold water; shake off excess water and chill 10 minutes.

MOST OF US GROW UP AND GET MARRIED,
BUT NOT ALL OF US IN THAT ORDER.

FRIES

You don't need a deep fryer for this recipe - just cut up the potatoes and bake.

2	2	**large baker potatoes**
2 tsp	10 mL	**vegetable oil**
¼ tsp	1.2 mL	**salt**
(optional)		**ketchup**

- Preheat oven to 400°F (200°C).
- Scrub potatoes and cut in quarters lengthwise; cut lengthwise into strips, French fry size.
- In a medium mixing bowl, with half the oil, toss potato strips until coated.
- Grease a cookie sheet with remaining vegetable oil and spread potatoes evenly over it; sprinkle with salt.
- Bake, turning once, for 20 - 25 minutes or until tender crisp.
- Serve hot, with ketchup (if desired).

GOING SHOPPING

2	2	baker potatoes (large)
¾ oz	21 g	celery
6 oz	170 g	cooked shrimp (small)
4	4	fresh bread slices
2	2	lettuce leaves
1 oz	28 g	onion

Check Your Shelves For:
butter or margarine
creamy cucumber dressing and dip mix
ketchup (optional)
lemon juice
mayonnaise
salt
vegetable oil

COOKING IT UP

Chicken in a hot creamy sauce, served over patty shells, is complemented by the cool, crisp, tangy taste of the salad.

CHICKEN ROYALE

3	3	large patty shells
2 tbsp	30 mL	butter or margarine
2 tbsp	30 mL	chopped green pepper
6	6	very small mushrooms
½ cup	125 mL	milk
2 tbsp	30 mL	corn starch
5 oz	142 mL	condensed chicken broth soup
1½ cups	375 mL	chopped cooked chicken
1 oz	28 mL	bottled sliced pimento, drained

- Place patty shells on 2 plates; remove tops and set alongside.
- In a medium saucepan, over medium heat, melt butter or margarine; add green pepper and mushrooms.
- Cook, stirring occasionally, for 3 minutes.
- Combine milk and corn starch and add, with remaining ingredients, to cooked green pepper and mushrooms.
- Reduce heat to medium/low and continue cooking, stirring frequently, for 5 minutes or until sauce thickens and chicken is well heated.
- Spoon into patty shells (this will likely overflow) and serve at once.

P.S.
Leftover soup can be frozen for future use.

Don't worry if you're in a hurry and haven't time to get the patty shells - you can serve this over buttered toast too.

COURTSHIP - THAT TIME IN LIFE
WHEN A MAN CHASES A WOMAN
UNTIL SHE CATCHES HIM.

CABBAGE AND APPLE MIX

1 tbsp	15 mL	granulated sugar
dash	dash	salt
3 tbsp	45 mL	mayonnaise
1 cup	250 mL	fresh shredded cabbage
1	1	medium McIntosh apple

- In a small mixing bowl, combine sugar, salt, mayonnaise and shredded cabbage.
- Wash, core and grate apple.
- Add to cabbage mixture and mix well.
- Cover with plastic wrap and refrigerate until ready to serve.

GOING SHOPPING

1 oz	28 mL	bottled sliced pimento
5 oz	142 mL	condensed chicken broth soup
10 oz	284 g	*cooked chicken
2 oz	57 g	fresh shredded cabbage
1 oz	28 g	green pepper
1	1	McIntosh apple (medium)
6	6	mushrooms (very small)
3	3	patty shells (large)

Check Your Shelves For:
butter or margarine
corn starch
granulated sugar
mayonnaise
milk
salt

---

* Refer to Monday - Week 1, page 20 or order from the Deli.

COOKING IT UP

SUNDAY - WEEK 4 No cooking time

Breakfast in bed, served on a tray - who could resist the pleasure of such a special treat? A perfect way to start the day with your sweetheart!

FRESH STRAWBERRIES (pictured on page 71)
12	12	large fresh strawberries

- Rinse strawberries in cold water; shake off excess water (do not remove stems).
- Serve in a pretty bowl.

P.S.
For best flavor and texture in strawberries, do not wash until just before serving.

RAISIN TEA BISCUITS (pictured on page 71)
2	2	raisin tea biscuits
2 tbsp	30 mL	spreadable cream cheese
4	4	dollops strawberry jelly

- Cut tea biscuits in half and lightly toast.
- Spread with cream cheese.
- Top with strawberry jelly and serve.

DID YOU KNOW?

Wearing a wedding ring on the third finger of the left hand is a very old custom. Ancient Egyptians believed a blood vessel in this finger (the "vena amoris") was connected directly to the heart. Since love was thought to be controlled by the heart, this finger was the one that held the ring as a pledge of love.

<u>DELICIOUS COFFEE</u> (pictured on page 71)

1 oz	28 g	Cappuccino instant coffee
10 oz	300 mL	hot water
2	2	dollops whipped topping

- Prepare coffee as directed and pour into 2 decorative coffee cups.
- Top with dollops of whipped topping just before serving.

GOING SHOPPING

1 oz	28 g	Cappuccino instant coffee
12	12	fresh strawberries (large)
2	2	raisin tea biscuits
2 oz	57 g	spreadable cream cheese
2 oz	57 g	whipped topping
(optional)		serving tray

<u>Check Your Shelves For</u>:
strawberry jelly

P.S.
To cut costs, check for day olds at your grocery store.

MOST MARRIAGES ARE NOT MADE IN
HEAVEN; THEY COME IN HIS AND HER
KITS THAT HAVE TO BE PUT TOGETHER.

NOTES

SWEET THINGS

(TOP SHELF, LEFT TO RIGHT)
RASPBERRY SURPRISE, page 103
GINGERBREAD VALENTINE, page 146
BLUEBERRY COBBLER, page 95
NUT CLUSTERS, page 132

(BOTTOM SHELF, LEFT TO RIGHT)
CHRISTMAS LIGHT COOKIES, page 96
CHRISTMAS TORTE, page 124

LOOKING IT OVER

SWEET THINGS

Almond Ice Cream
Apple In A Pie
Applesauce

Banana Custard
Black Forest Impression
Blueberry Cobbler
Bread Pudding

Christmas Light Cookies
Coconut Cream Bake
Creamy Chocolate Cheesecakes

Gingersnap Log

Hawaiian Cheesecakes

Krispie Rainbow Treats

Malt
Maple Pears
Mystery Confection

SWEET THINGS
(continued)

Pan Fried Apple
Peach Delight
Peanut Butter Crunch
Puffed Wheat Squares

Raisin Pears
Raspberry Surprise

S'mores
Strawberry Delight
Sundae Special

Whipped Cream

SWEET THINGS

All of the following recipes serve two. When choosing these desserts, remember to include the ingredients in your Going Shopping amounts.

ALMOND ICE CREAM

2	2	scoops vanilla ice cream
2 tbsp	30 mL	butterscotch flavor topping
2 tsp	10 mL	ground almonds
¼ tsp	1.2 mL	ground cinnamon

- Put ice cream into 2 dessert dishes.
- Spoon butterscotch topping over ice cream.
- To serve, top with almonds and sprinkle with cinnamon.

APPLE IN A PIE

A unique treat - pie crust is formed around a stuffed apple.

¼ cup	60 mL	quick oats
¼ cup	60 mL	packed brown sugar
pinch	pinch	ground nutmeg
½ tsp	2.5 mL	ground cinnamon
2 tbsp	30 mL	butter or margarine, softened
2	2	small McIntosh apples
2	2	*mini pie shells, thawed
(optional)		vanilla ice cream

- Preheat oven to 350°F (180°C).
- In a small bowl, combine oats, sugar, nutmeg and cinnamon; with fork or fingers, blend in butter or margarine until mixture is crumbly.
- Peel and core apples (do not slice) and place on pie shells.
- Pack oat mixture into centre and around base of apples.
- Fold edges of pie shells up and around apples to form a ball.
- Place on a pizza pan and bake 30 minutes or until pie shells are golden and apples are soft.
- Place on 2 small plates; top with ice cream (if desired) and serve.

  * If mini pie shells are unavailable, use a regular pie shell cut in half.

APPLESAUCE

For the apple of your eye!

2	2	medium McIntosh apples
3 tbsp	45 mL	water
dash	dash	ground cinnamon
1 tbsp	15 mL	brown sugar

- Peel, core and thinly slice apples.
- In a small saucepan, over medium heat, bring apple slices and water to a boil.
- Reduce heat to medium/low, cover and simmer 12 - 15 minutes or until apples are very tender.
- With potato masher, mash apples and spoon into 2 dessert dishes.
- Cool slightly, sprinkle with cinnamon and sugar and serve.

A MARRIED MAN LEARNS TO HANDLE MANY
PROBLEMS...SOME THAT HE WOULDN'T HAVE
IF HE HADN'T MARRIED IN THE FIRST PLACE.

BANANA CUSTARD

Like banana cream pie, but much faster.

1 tbsp	15 mL	custard powder
1 tbsp	15 mL	sugar
½ cup	125 mL	milk
1	1	small banana, sliced
2	2	single serve graham shells

- In a small saucepan, combine custard powder and sugar and slowly mix in milk.
- Cook and stir over medium heat for 3 minutes or until mixture thickens and comes to a full boil.
- Put banana slices in bottom of graham shells and pour custard over; top with 1 slice of banana on each.
- Chill 5 minutes and serve.

BLACK FOREST IMPRESSION

You'll be impressed when you taste this easy version of Black Forest cake.

1 cup	250 mL	chocolate baking crumbs
1¼ cups	310 mL	*whipped cream
½ cup	125 mL	canned cherry pie filling
⅛ tsp	.6 mL	artificial rum extract

- In a small mixing bowl, combine chocolate baking crumbs with 1 cup (250 mL) whipped cream.
- Spoon half the crumb mixture into the bottom of 2 ramekins.
- Combine cherry pie filling and rum extract; spread over crumb mixture.
- Top with remaining crumb mixture and then remaining whipped cream; garnish with a dollop of pie filling.
- This can be eaten right away, but tastes best if lightly covered with plastic wrap and chilled 4 hours before serving.

  * See Whipped Cream, page 105.

P.S.
Leftover cherry or blueberry pie filling can be used in place of cranberry sauce in Cranberry Squares, see Something Special - Coffee and Dessert, page 129.

BLUEBERRY COBBLER (pictured on page 89)

½ cup	125 mL	Harvest Crunch original blend granola cereal
½ cup	125 mL	canned blueberry pie filling
1 cup	250 mL	whipped topping

- Put half the granola and then half the pie filling into 2 dessert dishes; repeat with remaining granola and pie filling.
- Gently spread on whipped topping and garnish with a dollop of pie filling.
- Chill at least 4 hours before serving.

P.S.
Whipped topping will be more manageable if you soften before using.

BREAD PUDDING

1 cup	250 mL	cinnamon bun cut into cubes
1 cup	250 mL	hot milk
1 tbsp	15 mL	granulated sugar
1 tsp	5 mL	butter or margarine
pinch	pinch	salt
1	1	large egg, fork-beaten
¼ tsp	1.2 mL	vanilla
(optional)		light cream

- Preheat oven to 350°F (180°C).
- In a small mixing bowl, soak cinnamon bun in hot milk for 5 minutes.
- Add remaining ingredients, except cream; mix well.
- Pour into 2 greased ramekins and bake 1 hour or until knife inserted in centre comes out clean.
- Serve warm (with cream, if desired).

CHRISTMAS LIGHT COOKIES (pictured on page 89)

1½ tbsp	22.5 mL	butter or margarine
3 tbsp	45 mL	brown sugar
2 tbsp	30 mL	granulated sugar
¼ tsp	1.2 mL	baking soda
¼ tsp	1.2 mL	vanilla
¼ cup	60 mL	crunchy peanut butter
1	1	large egg
1 cup	250 mL	quick oats
¼ cup	60 mL	semi-sweet chocolate chips
2 tbsp	30 mL	color coated chocolate candies

- Preheat oven to 350°F (180°C).
- In a small mixing bowl, with mixer at medium speed, combine butter or margarine, sugars, soda, vanilla, peanut butter and egg; stir in oats and chocolate chips.
- Form 2 balls; flatten and shape into 2 round cookies ½" (1.5 cm) thick.
- Press in candies at various places.
- Place on a cookie sheet and bake 12 - 15 minutes or until brown around the edges.
- Cool completely before removing from cookie sheet to avoid breaking.

COCONUT CREAM BAKE

3 tbsp	45 mL	biscuit mix
3 tbsp	45 mL	granulated sugar
1	1	large egg
¾ cup	185 mL	milk
¼ tsp	1.2 mL	vanilla
1 tbsp	15 mL	butter or margarine
¼ cup	60 mL	sweet fancy flake coconut
(optional)		vanilla ice cream

- Preheat oven to 400°F (200°C).
- In a small mixing bowl, with mixer at medium speed, combine all ingredients, except coconut and ice cream, and blend 1 minute; hand stir in coconut.
- Pour into 2 greased ramekins.
- Bake 25 minutes or until set.
- Serve warm (topped with ice cream, if desired).

P.S.
Butter or margarine is easier to work with if softened.

CREAMY CHOCOLATE CHEESECAKES

1 tbsp	15 mL	butter, melted
¼ cup	60 mL	chocolate baking crumbs
3 oz	85 g	spreadable cream cheese
¾ cup	185 mL	whipped topping
2 tbsp	30 mL	semi-sweet chocolate chips

- In a small bowl, combine butter and chocolate baking crumbs; firmly press into the bottom of 2 ramekins.
- In a small mixing bowl, with mixer at medium speed, combine cream cheese and whipped topping.
- In a small saucepan, stirring continuously to prevent sticking, melt chocolate chips; remove from heat and spoon onto cream cheese mixture.
- With a knife, stir the chocolate into the cream cheese mixture in a circular fashion, stirring just enough to create a marbled effect.
- Spoon mixture over chocolate baking crumbs.
- Cover with plastic wrap and chill 1 hour or until set.

GINGERSNAP LOG

½ cup	125 mL	heavy or whipping cream
2 tsp	10 mL	granulated sugar
½ tsp	2.5 mL	lemon extract
12	12	thin gingersnap cookies
½ tsp	2.5 mL	lemon peel spice

- In a small mixing bowl, with mixer at medium speed, beat cream just until medium peaks form (over-beating will turn cream to butter).
- Stir in sugar and lemon extract.
- Spread about 1 tsp (5 mL) whipped cream on each gingersnap cookie.
- Stack the cookies horizontally to form a log; spread top and sides with remaining whipped cream.
- Sprinkle with lemon peel spice.
- Put 3 toothpicks partially into log and gently drape with plastic wrap.
- Chill 4 hours or until cookies soften.
- Cut diagonally in half and serve.

HAWAIIAN CHEESECAKES

It's the pineapple taste that makes these cheesecakes special.

1 tbsp	15 mL	butter, melted
¼ cup	60 mL	graham crumbs
3 oz	85 g	spreadable cream cheese
1 tbsp	15 mL	granulated sugar
5 oz	142 g	canned diced pineapple, drained
¾ cup	185 mL	whipped topping

- In a small bowl, combine butter and graham crumbs; firmly press into the bottom of 2 ramekins.
- In a small mixing bowl, with mixer at medium speed, combine remaining ingredients.
- Spoon over graham crumbs.
- Cover with plastic wrap and chill 1 hour or until set.

P.S.
You'll find baking or cooking is a lot more fun if you work together - you'll have more time to enjoy each other's company too.

KRISPIE RAINBOW TREATS

This colorful recipe has a chocolaty taste - a favorite for every age!

2 tbsp	30 mL	miniature colored baking chips
1 tbsp	15 mL	butter or margarine
1 cup	250 mL	miniature marshmallows
2	2	drops vanilla
1¼ cups	310 mL	crisp rice cereal

- **Put baking chips in the freezer for 30 minutes just before using.**
- In a small saucepan, over medium/low heat, while stirring, melt butter or margarine and marshmallows.
- Remove from heat; stir in vanilla and crisp rice cereal.
- Cool 2 minutes and carefully stir in baking chips (do not over-mix or colors will run together).
- Gently shape into 2 balls; cool completely and serve.

P.S.
To keep mixture from sticking to utensils or hands while mixing and shaping, grease with butter or margarine first.

MALT

1 qt	1 L	vanilla ice cream
½ cup	125 mL	milk
1 tbsp	15 mL	malt drink mix
2 tbsp	30 mL	chocolate syrup

- In a small mixing bowl, with mixer at medium speed, combine ice cream, milk, malt drink mix and chocolate syrup.
- Beat 30 seconds or just until blended (do not over-beat).
- Pour into 2 tall glasses and serve with straws and long spoons.

A WOMAN WORRIES ABOUT THE FUTURE
BEFORE SHE GETS A HUSBAND.
A MAN WORRIES ABOUT THE FUTURE
AFTER HE GETS A WIFE.

MAPLE PEARS

A simple dessert - takes only minutes to prepare.

14 oz	398 mL	canned pear slices, drained
¼ cup	60 mL	spreadable cream cheese
1 tbsp	15 mL	icing or confectioners' sugar
1 tbsp	15 mL	heavy or whipping cream
3	3	drops maple extract
1 tsp	5 mL	finely chopped pecans

- Put pears in 2 dessert dishes.
- In a small mixing bowl, with mixer at medium speed, beat cream cheese, sugar, cream and maple extract for 2 minutes.
- Spoon over pears and sprinkle with pecans.
- This can be served right away, but tastes good cooled too.

MYSTERY CONFECTION

For a treat that's "out of this world" try this recipe.

1⅛ oz	32 g	*chocolate covered candy bar with a chewy caramel filling
1½ tbsp	22.5 mL	butter or margarine
½ cup	125 mL	crisp rice cereal
½ cup	125 mL	semi-sweet chocolate chips

- In a small saucepan, over medium/low heat, stirring constantly to prevent burning, heat candy bar and butter or margarine for 5 minutes or until completely melted and smooth.
- Remove from heat and stir in crisp rice cereal.
- With a buttered spoon, pack mixture evenly into a **well-greased** mini fruit pan.
- In the same small saucepan, over medium/low heat, stirring constantly to prevent sticking, melt chocolate chips.
- Spread over candy bar mixture and chill 1 hour or until top is set.
- Gently loosen and turn out of pan; thaw 15 minutes, cut in half and serve.

* Various types of candy bar will work in this recipe, so try some different ones.

PAN FRIED APPLE

1	1	large Golden Delicious apple
2 tsp	10 mL	butter or margarine
2 tbsp	30 mL	maple syrup
2	2	scoops vanilla ice cream
2 tsp	10 mL	chopped pecans

- Core and cut apple in ½" (12 mm) wedges.
- In a small frying pan, over medium heat, fry apple wedges in butter or margarine, stirring occasionally, for 5 minutes or until lightly browned; reduce heat to medium/low, cover and cook another 10 minutes or until tender.
- Remove from heat and stir in maple syrup.
- Put ice cream into 2 dessert dishes; top with apples and sauce mixture and sprinkle with nuts.
- Serve at once.

PEACH DELIGHT

14 oz	398 mL	canned peach slices
2 tbsp	30 mL	bread crumbs
3 tbsp	45 mL	all purpose flour
4 tsp	20 mL	brown sugar
¼ tsp	1.2 mL	ground cinnamon
2 tbsp	30 mL	butter or margarine, softened
2 tbsp	30 mL	finely chopped pecans
(optional)		vanilla ice cream

- Preheat oven to 400°F (200°C).
- Drain peach slices, saving 2 tbsp (30 mL) syrup.
- Spoon fruit into 2 ramekins and add the reserved syrup.
- In a small mixing bowl, combine bread crumbs, flour, sugar and cinnamon.
- With fork or fingers, blend butter or margarine into bread mixture until large crumbs form; stir in pecans.
- Sprinkle crumb mixture over peaches and bake 15 - 20 minutes or until topping is browned.
- Serve warm (with ice cream, if desired).

PEANUT BUTTER CRUNCH

¼ cup	60 mL	graham crumbs
2 tsp	10 mL	brown sugar
2 tsp	10 mL	butter, melted
1½ cups	375 mL	vanilla ice cream, softened
2 tbsp	30 mL	extra crunchy peanut butter
2 tsp	10 mL	chocolate syrup

- In a small bowl, combine graham crumbs, sugar and melted butter.
- Press mixture firmly into the bottom of 2 ramekins and chill 30 minutes.
- In a small mixing bowl, combine ice cream and peanut butter; spoon over prepared graham crust.
- Freeze 30 minutes or until hardened.
- Just before serving, top with chocolate syrup.

PUFFED WHEAT SQUARES

¼ cup	60 mL	granulated sugar
¼ cup	60 mL	corn syrup
1 tbsp	15 mL	cocoa
4 tsp	20 mL	butter or margarine
2½ cups	625 mL	puffed wheat

- In a small saucepan, over medium heat, combine sugar, syrup, cocoa and butter or margarine.
- Cook, stirring to prevent sticking, for 2 - 3 minutes or until mixture comes to a boil; continue cooking and stirring 1 more minute.
- Remove from heat, add puffed wheat and stir to coat.
- Press mixture into a mini fruit cake pan.
- Cool, remove from pan and cut in half before serving.

P.S.
If you're not serving these right away, covering them with plastic wrap will keep them chewy; if you prefer them crunchy, leave uncovered.

LOVE: MUTUAL ADMIRATION SOCIETY

RAISIN PEARS

This is nice either to finish a meal or as a semi-sweet side dish with the main course.

14 oz	398 mL	canned pear slices
1 tbsp	15 mL	corn starch
1 tbsp	15 mL	brown sugar
2 tbsp	30 mL	golden seedless raisins

- Drain pears, saving the juice.
- In a small saucepan, over medium heat, combine corn starch, sugar and the juice from the pears.
- Cook, while stirring, for 1 minute or until sauce begins to thicken.
- Gently add pear slices and raisins.
- Reduce heat to medium/low and cook, stirring occasionally, 5 minutes longer.
- Spoon into 2 dessert dishes and serve warm.

RASPBERRY SURPRISE (pictured on page 89)

Eating this is like finding a buried treasure at the bottom of your glass.

6 oz	170 g	raspberry yogurt
1½ oz	42 g	strawberry jelly powder
½ cup	125 mL	boiling water
½ cup	125 mL	ice cubes
¼ cup	60 mL	*whipped cream
2	2	cocktail cherries

- Spoon the yogurt into 2 parfait glasses.
- In a medium mixing bowl, combine jelly powder and boiling water; stir 2 minutes or until jelly is completely dissolved.
- Stir in ice and chill 30 minutes or until jelly begins to thicken.
- Pour over yogurt; chill again for 1 hour or until jelly sets.
- To serve, spoon on whipped cream and top with cocktail cherries.

* See Whipped Cream, page 105.

S'MORES

Gooey & delicious - so good, you'll want s'more.

8	8	graham wafers
4	4	squares of a thin milk chocolate bar
4	4	regular marshmallows

- Preheat broiler, if manufacturer directs.
- Place 4 graham wafers on a cookie sheet.
- Top each wafer with a square of chocolate and then a marshmallow.
- Put cookie sheet on the second shelf under the broiler; broil 2 minutes or until the marshmallow toasts and is melting.
- Remove from oven and cover with second wafer, pressing down.
- Cool slightly before eating.

P.S.
These are fun to make around a camp fire. You can roast the marshmallows over the fire instead of broiling them; the hot marshmallow then melts the chocolate.

STRAWBERRY DELUXE

16	16	fresh strawberries
1 tbsp	15 mL	custard powder
1 tbsp	15 mL	sugar
½ cup	125 mL	milk
2	2	drops vanilla

- Wash strawberries and remove stems; place in 2 dessert dishes.
- In a small saucepan, combine custard powder and sugar; gradually stir in milk.
- Cook and stir over medium/high heat for 3 - 5 minutes or until mixture thickens.
- Remove from heat, stir in vanilla and pour over strawberries.
- Serve warm.

MARRIAGES MAY BE MADE IN HEAVEN, BUT
YOU'RE IN CHARGE OF MAINTENANCE HERE.

SUNDAE SPECIAL

2	2	scoops vanilla ice cream
¼ cup	60 mL	marshmallow creme topping
½ tsp	2.5 mL	very hot water
2 tbsp	30 mL	crushed candy cane

- Put ice cream into 2 dessert dishes.
- In a small bowl, blend marshmallow creme topping and water; spoon over ice cream.
- Top with crushed candy and serve at once.

P.S.
Put candy cane in a plastic bag before crushing.

NOWADAYS, IT DOESN'T SEEM TO MATTER WHO
WEARS THE PANTS IN THE FAMILY, JUST AS
LONG AS THERE'S MONEY IN THE POCKETS.

WHIPPED CREAM

½ pt	250 mL	heavy or whipping cream
1 tbsp	15 mL	granulated sugar
½ tsp	2.5 mL	vanilla

- In a small mixing bowl, with mixer at medium speed, beat cream just until medium peaks form (over-beating will turn cream to butter).
- Stir in sugar and vanilla.
- Serve as topping or make whipped cream dollops by dropping spoonfuls of whipped cream onto foil and freezing; when frozen, transfer dollops to plastic bag and store in freezer.
- Thaw dollops about 20 minutes before using.

P.S.
Cream almost doubles in size when whipped. Whipped cream can be used in place of whipped topping in all of the above Sweet Things recipes.

NOTES

ANNIVERSARY

BROILED LOBSTER TAILS, page 112
APPLE NUT RICE, page 111
BROCCOLI CRISPS, page 111

ANTIQUE DISHES COURTESY OF MARIE SCHATZ

LOOKING IT OVER

SOMETHING SPECIAL

ANNIVERSARY
(Serves 2)
Broiled Lobster Tails
Apple Nut Rice
Broccoli Crisps
Ice Cream Parfait

BIRTHDAY
(Serves 6)
Roast Beef
Yorkshire Pudding
New Potatoes
Glazed Onions
Beets à la Orange
Carrot Cake

CHRISTMAS
(Serves 6)
Cabbage Rolls
Perogie Casserole
Ukrainian Sausage
Nippy Carrots
Bean Salad
Christmas Torte

COFFEE & DESSERT
(Serves 6)
Coffee and
Chocolate Fondue or
Cranberry Squares or
Pineapple Delight or
Pumpkin Slice or
Nut Clusters

SOMETHING SPECIAL
(continued)

EASTER
(Serves 6)
Baked Ham
Sweet Potatoes
Green Beans Supreme
Marbled Eggs
Palm Sundae

THANKSGIVING
(Serves 6)
Roast Turkey Breast
Stuffing
Mashed Potatoes
Scalloped Corn
Cranberry Salad
Frosty Pumpkin Pie
Iced Tea

VALENTINE'S DAY
(Serves 2)
Peppercorn Steak
Baked Potatoes
Zucchini and Red Pepper
Lettuce Alone Salad
Cheese Toast
Gingerbread Valentine
Raspberry Kiss

SOMETHING SPECIAL

ANNIVERSARY Serves 2

Many newlyweds look forward to a romantic evening on their wedding anniversary. And what could be more romantic than a dinner for two in front of a cozy fire. This special meal captures the excitement of the day.

APPLE NUT RICE (pictured on page 107)

1 cup	250 mL	water
¼ cup	60 mL	apple juice
¼ tsp	1.2 mL	salt
1 tbsp	15 mL	butter or margarine
½ cup	125 mL	long grain and wild rice
1	1	small McIntosh apple, peeled, cored and chopped
¼ cup	60 mL	chopped brazil nuts

- In a small saucepan, combine water, apple juice, salt and butter or margarine.
- Bring to a boil over medium heat; stir in rice.
- Cover, reduce heat to low and simmer 20 minutes.
- Stir in apples and nuts and simmer 5 more minutes or until liquid is absorbed.
- Fluff with a fork before serving.

BROCCOLI CRISPS (pictured on page 107)

2 cups	500 mL	broccoli flowerets
2 cups	500 mL	boiling water
2 tbsp	30 mL	butter or margarine
2 tsp	10 mL	lemon cheese spread

- Rinse broccoli with boiling water; drain well.
- In a small saucepan, combine all ingredients.
- Cook and stir over medium heat, for 5 minutes or until broccoli is tender crisp.
- Serve at once.

Sparkling Red Grape Juice is a tasty complement to this meal.

BROILED LOBSTER TAILS (pictured on page 107)

6	6	small rock lobster tails
3 tbsp	45 mL	butter, melted

- **If using frozen lobster tails, thaw in the fridge for 8 hours.**
- Preheat broiler, if manufacturer suggests.
- With kitchen shears, cut away thin underside from shell and discard; gently pull meat from shell.
- With a sharp knife, cut along backside of meat, about ¼" (6 mm) deep, to expose dark vein; remove and discard.
- Return meat to shells.
- Place tails, shell side up, on rack in broiling pan and place pan 7" (18 cm) from heat source.
- Broil 6 minutes; turn and broil meat side 5 more minutes or until meat is opaque.
- Serve in shell, with small dishes of hot melted butter for dipping meat.

Ice Cream Parfait makes a nice finish to this meal, or you may wish to serve your wedding cake, if you have some saved.

MEMORY - SOMETHING THAT TELLS A MAN
HE'S FORGOTTEN HIS ANNIVERSARY.

ICE CREAM PARFAIT

4	4	scoops vanilla ice cream
2 tbsp	30 mL	creme de menthe syrup
¼ cup	60 mL	whipped topping
2	2	maraschino cherries

- Put ice cream into 2 parfait glasses.
- Pour creme de menthe syrup over.
- Top with whipped topping and maraschino cherries.
- Serve with 2 long spoons.

35 minutes ahead	- cook **Apple Nut Rice**
11 minutes ahead (thawed)	- broil **Lobster Tails**
10 minutes ahead	- make **Broccoli Crisps**

DID YOU KNOW?

Wedding cakes weren't always for eating - at one time, they were made for throwing! In the 18th century, small cakes were baked, crumbled and then tossed at the bride and groom. It was believed that couples hit by many of these pieces of cake would be blessed with many children.

Throwing rice or bird seed at the bride and groom comes from another old custom. In some places, cereal grains were thrown at the "just married" couple with the belief that if they were hit by many of these grains they would be guaranteed a large family.

AN EXERCISE SURE TO CHANGE YOUR
LIFE IS WALKING DOWN THE ISLE.

GOING SHOPPING

2 oz	60 mL	apple juice
6 oz	170 g	*broccoli flowerets
1	1	McIntosh apple (small)
12 oz	341 g	rock lobster tails
24 oz	660 mL	sparkling red grape juice
8 oz	250 mL	vanilla ice cream
2 oz	60 mL	whipped topping

Check Your Shelves For:
butter and/or margarine
chopped brazil nuts
creme de menthe syrup
lemon cheese spread
long grain and wild rice
maraschino cherries
salt

---

* *If you are purchasing broccoli with the stalks, you will need to double the weight required.*

Customarily, a paper gift is given on the first anniversary. Following are some of the other major dates and gifts:

5th year - wood

10th year - tin

15th year - crystal

20th year - china

25th year - silver

50th year - gold

SOMETHING SPECIAL

BIRTHDAY Serves 6

Each family and each culture has its own traditions for celebrating birthdays. In China, New Year's Day is a "giant birthday party" - everyone becomes a year older then.

Here in North America, a birthday is usually an occasion for family and friends to gather. Here is an all-time favorite meal for such a celebration.

ROAST BEEF
4¼ lbs	1.9 kg	prime rib roast
1 tsp	5 mL	salt
¼ tsp	1.2 mL	pepper

- Preheat oven to 325°F (165°C).
- Place meat in a roasting pan, fat side up; sprinkle with salt and pepper.
- Insert meat thermometer into thickest part of roast, making sure it is not resting on fat.
- Roast 3 hours or until thermometer reaches 160°F (71°C) for medium beef or 170°F (77°C) for well done.
- Remove from oven, slice and serve on a warm platter.

GLAZED ONIONS
1½ lbs	681 g	pearl onions
½ cup	125 mL	beef drippings

- Preheat oven to 325°F (165°C).
- Peel outer skin from onions, leaving a little of the root ends to help hold their shape.
- Place in a roasting pan with beef drippings and turn to coat.
- Cook 30 minutes or until fork-tender.
- Remove from oven and serve.

P.S.
If making Glazed Onions at the same time as roast beef, add to pan during the last 30 minutes; remove from oven and serve along-side meat.

To easily peel onions, place in boiling water for 3 minutes and then rinse in cold water. When choosing this method for peeling, reduce cooking time to 15 minutes.

NEW POTATOES

12	12	medium new red potatoes
1 tsp	5 mL	salt
		hot water (to cover)

- Scrub potatoes and peel a thin strip around the centre of each one.
- In a large saucepan, over high heat, bring potatoes to a boil in salted water.
- Reduce heat to medium/low, cover and simmer 1½ hours or until fork-tender; drain.
- Transfer to a vegetable bowl, cover and keep warm until ready to serve.

P.S.
You may want to save the water drained from potatoes to use when making gravy as it makes gravy tastier.

BEEF GRAVY

5 tbsp	75 mL	*beef drippings
5 tbsp	75 mL	all purpose flour
¼ oz	5 g	instant beef bouillon
2 cups	500 mL	water (approximately)
(to taste)		salt
(to taste)		pepper

- In a roasting pan or large frying pan, over medium heat, blend beef drippings with flour and beef bouillon.
- Slowly add water, stirring until gravy reaches a pouring consistency; bring to a boil (add more water if gravy is too thick).
- Season with salt and pepper.
- Put in a gravy boat and serve.

* *If there isn't enough beef drippings, add butter or margarine.*

OPTIMIST - A BRIDEGROOM WHO
THINKS HE HAS NO BAD HABITS.

YORKSHIRE PUDDING

5¼ oz	149 g	yorkshire pudding mix
3	3	large eggs
1 cup	250 mL	milk or water
3 tbsp	45 mL	vegetable oil

- Preheat oven to 425°F (220°C).
- Prepare yorkshire pudding mix according to package directions.
- Pour vegetable oil into each section of a 12 unit muffin tin and tilt to coat the bottom; place in oven to preheat 5 minutes.
- Pour batter into muffin tin and bake 20 minutes or until risen and lightly browned (yorkshires will naturally fall as they cool).
- Serve hot.

P.S.
Make Yorkshires early in the day and reheat in a 325°F (165°C) oven for 10 minutes just before serving.

BEETS À LA ORANGE

1 tbsp	15 mL	butter or margarine
3 tbsp	45 mL	granulated sugar
1 tbsp	15 mL	cornstarch
1 tsp	5 mL	orange peel spice
3 tbsp	45 mL	orange juice
42 oz	1194 mL	canned sliced beets, drained

- In a medium saucepan, combine all ingredients, except beets.
- Cook and stir over medium heat for 3 minutes or until thickened.
- Add beets and continue cooking and gently stirring 2 minutes longer or until beets are well heated.
- Serve in a warmed vegetable bowl.

P.S.
Organize your refrigerator so that you store your leftovers together - that way you will easily see what has to be used quickly and avoid food waste.

The tradition in North America of putting candles on a birthday cake originated in Germany where it was the custom to put tiny candles on top of a cake, usually one candle for each year and one for the year to come.

CARROT CAKE

2 cups	500 mL	all purpose flour
2 cups	500 mL	granulated sugar
2 tsp	10 mL	baking powder
1 tsp	5 mL	baking soda
2 tsp	10 mL	ground nutmeg
1 tsp	5 mL	salt
1⅓ cups	335 mL	vegetable oil
4	4	large eggs
3 cups	750 mL	grated carrots
¼ cup	60 mL	chopped pecans
		non-stick cooking spray
(optional)		birthday candles

- Preheat oven to 350°F (180°C).
- In a large mixing bowl, combine dry ingredients.
- With mixer at low speed, mix in oil and eggs, scraping sides of bowl often; hand stir in carrots and pecans.
- Spray a bundt pan with cooking spray and spoon in cake mixture.
- Bake 55 minutes or until a toothpick inserted in middle comes out clean.
- Remove from oven and cool 10 minutes; remove from pan and cool completely.
- Spoon frosting (below) onto top of cake and encourage it to flow in grooves.
- Serve (with candles, if desired).

FROSTING

1 tsp	5 mL	butter or margarine
½ c	125 mL	spreadable cream cheese
1¼ cups	310 mL	icing or confectioners' sugar
½ tsp	2.5 mL	vanilla

- In a small mixing bowl, with mixer at medium speed, beat butter or margarine and cream cheese until softened.
- Mix in remaining ingredients.

day before	- make **Birthday Cake**
early in day	- make **Yorkshire Pudding**
3 hours ahead	- place **Roast** in oven
2 hours ahead	- put **Potatoes** on to cook
30 minutes ahead	- place **Onions** in oven
10 minutes ahead	- make **Gravy**
	- reheat **Yorkshire Pudding**
5 minutes ahead	- put **Beets** on to cook

DID YOU KNOW?

In centuries past, the best man's role was a little more involved than it is today. Stealing a bride in those days was an acceptable way of getting a wife and the groom needed a friend to help him. The friend or best man stayed by the groom's side during the wedding in case the bride's parents tried to take her back.

After the wedding, if the bride had been stolen, the groom often hid his 'honey' for a 'moon' to allow the anger of her parents to cool. So began the tradition of a honeymoon.

GOING SHOPPING

42 oz	1194 mL	canned sliced beets
1 lb	454 g	carrots
7	7	eggs (large)
12	12	new red potatoes (medium)
1½ oz	45 mL	orange juice
1½ lbs	681 g	pearl onions
4¼ lbs	1.9 kg	prime rib roast
4 oz	114 g	spreadable cream cheese
5¼ oz	149 g	yorkshire pudding mix

Check Your Shelves For:
all purpose flour
baking powder
baking soda
birthday candles (optional)
butter or margarine
cornstarch
granulated sugar
ground nutmeg
icing or confectioners' sugar
instant beef bouillon
milk (optional)
non-stick cooking spray
orange peel spice
pecan pieces
pepper
salt
vanilla
vegetable oil

SOMETHING SPECIAL

CHRISTMAS Serves 6

For something different, celebrate a Ukrainian Christmas Eve. While not a traditional meal, the following recipes have a Ukrainian flavor your guests are sure to enjoy.

Dinner begins just as the first star of the evening glimmers in the sky. The father recites the Lord's Prayer and then proclaims "Khrystos Rodyvsya" (Christ is born), and the family answers "Slavim Yoho" (Let us glorify Him).

CABBAGE ROLLS

1	1	medium head of cabbage
1 cup	250 mL	chopped onion
5 tbsp	75 mL	butter or margarine
8 oz	227 g	regular ground beef
1½ tsp	7.5 mL	salt
¼ tsp	1.2 mL	pepper
1 cup	250 mL	long grain rice, cooked
20 oz	568 mL	condensed tomato soup
3 tbsp	45 mL	apple cider vinegar
2 tbsp	30 mL	brown sugar

- To soften cabbage, remove core, wrap in foil and freeze 48 hours; thaw 8 hours, put in a deep container and cover with boiling water.
- Preheat oven to 350°F (180°C).
- Carefully remove cabbage from boiling water, separate leaves and pare veins (save larger leaves).
- In a large frying pan over medium heat, cook the onion in 3 tbsp (45 mL) of butter or margarine until tender; add ground beef and, stirring frequently, cook 5 minutes or until lightly browned.
- In a medium mixing bowl, combine the cooked onion and ground beef with salt, pepper and cooked rice.
- Put a generous spoonful of the meat mixture on a cabbage leaf, roll up and tuck in the ends; repeat until all mixture has been used.
- Line the bottom of a large greased casserole with a few of the larger leaves; arrange the cabbage rolls in layers in the casserole and dot with remaining butter or margarine.
- In a small mixing bowl, combine soup, vinegar and sugar; pour over cabbage rolls and cover with any remaining leaves.
- Cover and bake 1½ - 2 hours or until cabbage is tender.
- Serve hot.

PEROGIE CASSEROLE

4	4	large eggs, fork-beaten
1 tsp	5 mL	baking powder
1½ tsp	7.5 mL	seasoning salt
1 tsp	5 mL	prepared mustard
½ cup	125 mL	chopped onion
1⅔ lbs	757 g	cottage cheese, drained
6 oz	170 g	extra wide noodles, cooked
1½ cups	375 mL	grated mild cheddar cheese

- Preheat oven to 350°F (180°C).
- In a large mixing bowl, combine ingredients, saving half the cheddar cheese.
- Spoon mixture into a large, well-greased casserole and top with remaining cheese.
- Bake 1 hour or until top is firm.
- Serve with sauce (below).

SAUCE

3 tbsp	45 mL	butter
1 cup	250 mL	sour cream

- In a small saucepan, combine butter and sour cream.
- Cook and stir over medium heat for 4 minutes or until butter is melted and sauce is hot.
- Pour into a gravy boat.

UKRAINIAN SAUSAGE

20 oz	568 g	Ukrainian sausage

- Preheat oven to 350°F (180°C).
- If casing can be removed, peel sausage.
- Cut into 2" (5 cm) diagonal slices and place in a small casserole.
- Bake 45 minutes or until meat is browned and no longer pink inside.
- Serve hot.

NIPPY CARROTS

21 oz	596 g	frozen baby carrots
¼ cup	60 mL	cream of leek soup mix
¼ tsp	1.2 mL	salt
¾ cup	185 mL	milk

- Preheat oven to 350°F (180°C).
- Put carrots in a large casserole.
- In a small saucepan, combine soup mix, salt and milk.
- Cook over medium heat, stirring frequently, for 3 minutes or until soup thickens and comes to a boil; pour over carrots.
- Cover and bake, stirring occasionally, for 1 hour or until carrots are tender crisp.
- Serve hot.

BEAN SALAD

¼ cup	60 mL	fine granulated sugar
¼ cup	60 mL	vegetable oil
¼ cup	60 mL	vinegar
½ tsp	2.5 mL	salt
14 oz	398 mL	canned red kidney beans, drained
10 oz	284 mL	canned cut wax beans, drained
10 oz	284 mL	canned cut green beans, drained
2 oz	57 g	sliced onion, separated into rings

- In a large salad bowl, combine sugar, oil, vinegar and salt.
- Add all beans and onion; toss to thoroughly coat.
- Chill at least 4 hours.
- Drain excess liquid just before serving.

A **Braided Christmas Loaf** and **Sparkling Apple Juice** will add a pleasing touch to this meal - be sure to include them.

P.S.
To fill your house with a pleasing aroma, after cooking foods with a strong smell, sprinkle cinnamon on a cookie sheet and place in a warm oven for ½ hour.

You may want to try this recipe before preparing it for company, as different ovens, etc. could influence the outcome - well worth the effort because it tastes so good!

CHRISTMAS TORTE (pictured on page 89)

4	4	large egg whites
¼ tsp	1.2 mL	cream of tartar
1 cup	250 mL	fine granulated sugar
1 tbsp	15 mL	cornstarch
		non-stick cooking spray
3 cups	750 mL	*whipped cream
1 cup	250 mL	sliced strawberries
2	2	kiwi, peeled and sliced
1 tbsp	15 mL	slivered almonds

- Preheat oven to 275°F (140°C).
- In a medium metal or glass mixing bowl, with mixer at high speed, beat egg whites and cream of tartar until soft peaks form.
- While beating, slowly sprinkle in sugar.
- Continue beating, scraping sides of bowl often, until stiff glossy peaks form when beaters are stopped and slowly raised; beat in the cornstarch.
- Liberally spray a 9" (22 cm) springform pan with cooking spray and spoon batter evenly into it.
- Bake 2 hours or until crisp and lightly browned on the outside.
- Allow to cool completely (Torte may deflate) before **gently** removing from pan.
- Cover loosely and refrigerate until required.
- Before serving, spread with whipped cream and top with fruit and almonds.

* See Sweet Things - Whipped Cream, page 105 (omit sugar).

P.S.
Egg yolks can be stored in the freezer in small air-tight containers.

day before or early in day	- make **Christmas Torte**
4 hours ahead	- make **Bean Salad**
2 hours ahead	- place **Cabbage Rolls** in oven
1 hour ahead	- place **Nippy Carrots** in oven
	- place **Perogie Casserole** in oven
45 minutes ahead	- place **Ukrainian Sausage** in oven

After the meal, the Ukrainian family sings carols and then, at midnight, attends a special Christmas service to hear the story of the birth of Christ and how He came to give eternal life to all who would believe in Him.

DID YOU KNOW?

Bridal Shows were fashionable in the Ukraine as early as the 18th century. In those days, on the first day of summer, unmarried young women were dressed in their best and presented to eligible young bachelors during a Bride-show. The young men would look the young women over and each would choose a bride. A week later, interviews with both sets of parents would take place and a marriage arranged. Here in North America, a Bridal Show is for women who are already pledged to be married - a time for viewing gowns, tuxedos and other things pertaining to weddings.

GOING SHOPPING

52 oz	1.5 L	bottles sparkling apple juice
1	1	braided Christmas loaf
1	1	cabbage heads (medium)
10 oz	284 mL	canned cut green beans
10 oz	284 mL	canned cut wax beans
14 oz	398 mL	canned red kidney beans
20 oz	568 mL	condensed tomato soup
1⅔ lbs	757 g	cottage cheese
¾ oz	20 g	cream of leek soup mix
8	8	eggs (large)
21 oz	596 g	frozen baby carrots
12 oz	375 mL	heavy or whipping cream
2	2	kiwi
4½ oz	128 g	mild cheddar cheese
5¼ oz	149 g	onion
8 oz	227 g	regular ground beef
8 oz	250 mL	sour cream
3 oz	85 g	strawberries
20 oz	568 g	Ukrainian sausage

Check Your Shelves For:

apple cider vinegar	non-stick cooking spray
baking powder	pepper
brown sugar	prepared mustard
butter and/or margarine	salt
cornstarch	seasoning salt
cream of tartar	slivered almonds
extra wide noodles	vanilla
fine granulated sugar	vegetable oil
long grain rice	vinegar
milk	

SOMETHING SPECIAL

COFFEE AND DESSERT Serves 6

Not up to making a big meal? Invite your friends over for coffee and serve them chocolate fondue.

CHOCOLATE FONDUE

2	2	large bananas, sliced
(optional)		lemon juice
½	½	small honeydew melon, cut into bite-sized pieces
12 oz	341 g	strawberries, stems removed
8 oz	227 g	seedless green grapes, removed from stems
2	2	small mandarin oranges, sectioned
12	12	regular marshmallows
1 lb	454 g	semi-sweet chocolate chips
1 cup	250 mL	heavy or whipping cream

- Dip banana slices into lemon juice if not using right away (to keep from turning brown).
- Arrange fruit and marshmallows on a platter; cover with plastic wrap until ready to serve.
- In a medium saucepan, over very low heat, combine chocolate chips and cream; heat, stirring often, for 20 minutes or until chocolate melts and mixture is smooth.
- Transfer chocolate to a fondue pot or serving dish.
- Give each person a wooden pick or fondue fork for dipping fruit and marshmallows into chocolate.
- Serve with coffee (next page).

P.S.
Other types of fruit may be used as well.

BEING MARRIED SAVES A MAN A LOT OF
TIME MAKING UP HIS MIND ABOUT THINGS.

COFFEE, DRIP TYPE

1½ qt	1.5 L	cold water
2 tbsp	30 mL	extra fine grind coffee
(optional)		light cream
(optional)		granulated sugar

· Pour cold water into coffee maker reservoir.
· Place coffee in a filter and put in section through which water will pour.
· Serve hot, with cream and sugar (if desired).

P.S.
Use extra fine grind coffee if using a drip type coffee maker or regular grind if percolating.

---

1 hour ahead   - prepare **Fruit**
30 minutes ahead - make **Chocolate Dip**
15 minutes ahead - make **Coffee**

GOING SHOPPING

2	2	bananas (large)
8 oz	250 mL	heavy or whipping cream
½	½	honeydew melon (small)
(optional)		light cream
2	2	mandarin oranges (small)
8 oz	227 g	seedless green grapes
1 lb	454 g	semi-sweet chocolate chips
12 oz	341 g	strawberries

Check Your Shelves For:
extra fine grind coffee
granulated sugar (optional)
lemon juice (optional)
regular marshmallows
wooden picks or fondue forks

*Following are other company dessert suggestions that serve 6 (when choosing them, be sure to include the ingredients on your **Going Shopping** list).*

CRANBERRY SQUARES

1 cup	250 mL	quick oats
1 cup	250 mL	all purpose flour
½ cup	125 mL	packed brown sugar
pinch	pinch	baking soda
½ cup	125 mL	butter, softened
10 oz	284 mL	canned whole cranberry sauce
(optional)		vanilla ice cream

- Preheat oven to 350°F (180°C).
- In a small mixing bowl, combine oats, flour, sugar and soda; add butter and mix together with fork or fingers until crumbly.
- Firmly press half the crumb mixture into bottom of an 8" (20 cm) square cake pan.
- Spread with cranberry sauce; sprinkle with remaining crumbs and press down with a fork.
- Bake 45 minutes or until topping reaches a golden brown.
- Serve warm (with ice cream, if desired).

P.S.
The exact measurement of cranberry sauce in this recipe is not too important - a little more or less works just as well. This can also be cooled and cut into squares, if you prefer.

DID YOU KNOW?

In the past century, many brides walked to church for the wedding along with family and friends. The bride and her maids wore similar clothing to disguise her in case someone, perhaps an ex-suitor, tried to steal her along the way. Today, the bride is usually transported to the ceremony, but she and her bridesmaids still dress in similar fashion.

PINEAPPLE DELIGHT

This melt in your mouth dessert keeps well in the freezer - a good one to have on hand for unexpected company.

1¼ cup	310 mL	graham crumbs
5 tbsp	75 mL	butter or margarine, melted
6 tbsp	90 mL	butter, softened
1 cup	250 mL	icing or confectioners' sugar
1 tbsp	15 mL	*meringue dessert mix
1½ tbsp	22.5 mL	*warm water
8 oz	227 mL	canned crushed pineapple, drained
1½ cups	375 mL	**whipped cream

· In a small mixing bowl, combine graham crumbs and melted butter or margarine.
· Firmly press mixture into bottom of an 8" (20 cm) square cake pan.
· In a small mixing bowl, with mixer at medium speed, blend softened butter and icing or confectioners' sugar.
· Add meringue dessert mix and warm water, beating 2 minutes or until light and fluffy; spread over graham crust.
· Spread pineapple evenly over meringue mixture and top with whipped cream.
· Freeze a minimum of 2 hours or until required.
· To serve, thaw 30 minutes, cut into 6 squares and place on dessert plates.

* *Meringue dessert mix and warm water used as a substitute for 1 large egg.*

** *See Sweet Things - Whipped Cream, page 105 (omit sugar and vanilla).*

P.S.
Freezing 20 - 30 minutes between each layer makes the preparation of this dessert more manageable.

NEVER SHOUT AT ONE ANOTHER
...UNLESS
THE HOUSE IS BURNING DOWN.

PUMPKIN SLICE

¼ cup	60 mL	butter or margarine, softened
½ cup	125 mL	packed brown sugar
1	1	large egg
6 oz	170 g	canned pumpkin
½ cup	125 mL	all purpose flour
¼ tsp	1.2 mL	salt
¼ tsp	1.2 mL	baking soda
½ tsp	2.5 mL	baking powder
½ tsp	2.5 mL	ground cinnamon
pinch	pinch	ground ginger
pinch	pinch	ground nutmeg
		*frosting

- Preheat oven to 350°F (180°C).
- In a small mixing bowl, with mixer at medium speed, combine butter or margarine and sugar.
- Beat in egg and then pumpkin.
- Blend remaining ingredients, except frosting, and add to pumpkin mixture.
- Mix well and spoon evenly into greased 8" (20 cm) square cake pan.
- Bake 25 minutes or until toothpick inserted in middle comes out clean.
- Frost before serving.

* For frosting, see Something Special - Birthday, page 118 (make half the recipe).

P.S.
Leftover pumpkin can be used in Frosty Pumpkin Pie, see Something Special - Thanksgiving, page 141.

HE WHO GIVES IN WHEN HE IS
WRONG, IS WISE.

HE WHO GIVES IN WHEN HE IS
RIGHT, IS MARRIED.

Invite some friends over to play games and make candy. A fun ice breaker is called "Guess Who" - you'll only need paper and pencils for this one and you can join in too.

GUESS WHO

Equipment listed is for a game with 6 people but can easily be adapted for more.

6	6	pencils
18	18	small pieces of paper
6	6	larger sheets of paper (with numbers 1-18 written down the left side)

- Divide pencils and paper evenly between players.
- Players write down 3 true, but not well known, facts about themselves, 1 on each piece of small paper; papers are then folded and put into a container.
- As the papers are drawn from the container, they are sequentially numbered and read out loud.
- Players "guess who" wrote each one, writing down their guess next to the appropriate number on their large sheet of paper.
- When all papers have been read, they are read a second time and authors then identify themselves.
- Correct answers get 1 point and the person with the most points wins.

NUT CLUSTERS (pictured on page 89)

This candy recipe is always a treat. It also makes a nice gift in a decorative container, tied with a pretty ribbon.

2 tbsp	30 mL	butter or margarine
2 tbsp	30 mL	white corn syrup
⅔ cup	165 mL	granulated sugar
2 cups	500 mL	whole blanched almonds
½ tsp	2.5 mL	salt

- In a medium saucepan, over medium heat, combine butter or margarine, syrup and sugar.
- Heat, while stirring, for 2 minutes or until sugar is thoroughly melted.
- Add almonds; cook and stir 7 minutes or until syrup color is deep gold.
- Spread nut mixture on foil and sprinkle with salt.
- Cool completely and break into pieces.

SOMETHING SPECIAL

EASTER Serves 6

Easter, the day when the resurrection of Christ is celebrated.

Since earliest times, eggs have been associated with Easter as they are a symbol of new life. Coloring them is a favorite tradition for children (and adults too). A variation of colored eggs is marbled eggs, shown below.

MARBLED EGGS

6	6	large eggs
		cold water (to cover)
¼ cup	60 mL	soy sauce
2 tbsp	30 mL	vinegar
4	4	tea bags
3 tbsp	45 mL	mayonnaise
½ tsp	2.5 mL	Dijon mustard
1½ tsp	7.5 mL	relish

- In a medium saucepan, over medium/high heat, cover eggs with water and bring to a boil; reduce heat to low, cover and cook 10 minutes.
- Remove eggs with slotted spoon and rinse with cold water until cooled.
- With back of spoon, tap eggs gently all over to form cracks in shells.
- Add soy sauce, vinegar and tea bags to egg cooking water.
- Return eggs to water and return to a boil over medium/high heat.
- Reduce heat to low and continue cooking for another 30 minutes; cool.

- Remove shells and cut eggs in half lengthwise.
- Remove yolks and, in a small bowl, mash yolks with a fork.
- Add mayonnaise, mustard and relish; mix well.
- Stuff egg white centres with yolk mixture.
- Place on a platter; lightly cover with plastic wrap and refrigerate until ready to serve.

P.S.
When you entertain, record the date, who your guests were and what you served them in a memo book; it will help you with menu planning the next time they visit.

BAKED HAM

2½ lbs	1.13 kg	smoked Black Forest boneless ham
(to taste)		Dijon mustard

- Preheat oven to 350°F (180°C).
- In a medium casserole, bake ham 40 minutes or until well heated.
- Slice and return to casserole; cover and keep warm until ready to serve.
- Mustard should be served in a small dish alongside the ham.

P.S.
Leftover ham, if any, could be used for Ham and Potato Casserole, see Thursday - Week 1, page 26.

SWEET POTATOES

57 oz	1620 mL	canned cut sweet potatoes, drained
6 tbsp	90 mL	butter or margarine
4¼ tsp	21.2 mL	corn starch
¼ tsp	1.2 mL	ground ginger
1½ tsp	7.5 mL	orange peel spice
¼ cup	60 mL	brown sugar
¾ cup	185 mL	orange juice
1 tbsp	15 mL	flaked almonds

- Preheat oven to 350°F (180°C).
- Place potatoes in a medium casserole.
- In a small saucepan, mix together remaining ingredients, except almonds.
- Cook and stir over medium/high heat for 3 minutes or until mixture thickens and comes to a boil; pour over potatoes and sprinkle with almonds.
- Bake 40 minutes or until sauce is hot and bubbly.
- Serve at once.

MARRIAGE CAN BE A MUTUAL PARTNERSHIP
IF PARTNERS KNOW WHEN TO BE MUTE.

GREEN BEANS SUPREME

1 tsp	5 mL	salt
½ cup	125 mL	water
21 oz	596 g	frozen whole green beans
2 tbsp	30 mL	butter or margarine
1½ tbsp	22.5 mL	Hollandaise sauce mix
⅓ cup	85 mL	condensed chicken broth soup

- In a medium saucepan, over medium heat, bring salted water to a boil; add beans and return to a boil.
- Cook, gently stirring for even cooking, for 5 minutes or until tender crisp; drain and place in a preheated vegetable dish.
- While beans are cooking, in a small saucepan over medium/high heat, melt butter or margarine and blend in Hollandaise sauce mix.
- Add chicken broth and cook, while stirring, until mixture comes to a boil and thickens slightly (do not overcook).
- Remove from heat; pour over beans and serve.

Hot Cross Buns are popular at Easter time. They make a nice addition to this meal.

PALM SUNDAE

1 tbsp	15 mL	butter or margarine
4 tsp	20 mL	all purpose flour
¼ cup	60 mL	brown sugar
2 tbsp	30 mL	chopped pecans
5 tbsp	75 mL	water
½ tsp	2.5 mL	imitation rum extract
6	6	scoops vanilla ice cream
1 tbsp	15 mL	colored fancy coconut

- In a small saucepan, over medium heat, combine all ingredients, except ice cream and coconut.
- Cook mixture 3 minutes or until it comes to a boil and thickens; cool slightly.
- To serve, put scoops of ice cream in 6 dessert dishes, top with sauce and sprinkle with coconut.

Easter (continued)

earlier in the day - make **Marbled Eggs**
40 minutes ahead - place **Ham** in oven
                  - place **Sweet Potatoes** in oven
15 minutes ahead - make **Green Beans Supreme**

GOING SHOPPING

57 oz	1620 mL	canned cut sweet potatoes
2.6 oz	85 mL	condensed chicken broth soup
6	6	eggs (large)
21 oz	596 g	frozen whole green beans
6	6	hot cross buns
6 oz	185 mL	orange juice
2½ lbs	1.13 kg	smoked Black Forest boneless ham
16 oz	500 mL	vanilla ice cream

Check Your Shelves For:

all purpose flour	imitation rum extract
brown sugar	mayonnaise
butter or margarine	orange peel spice
colored fancy coconut	pecan pieces
corn starch	relish
Dijon mustard	salt
flaked almonds	soy sauce
ground ginger	tea bags
Hollandaise sauce mix	vinegar

SOMETHING SPECIAL

THANKSGIVING   Serves 6

A time for giving thanks and enjoying the company of family and friends.

Early settlers had to hunt for their meal before their celebrations could begin and most likely they ate venison, partridge or even beaver tail. Those lucky enough to have turkey would be serving wild gobbler and not the easy-to-make store bought bird as seen in the following recipe.

ROAST TURKEY BREAST

| 3½ lbs | 1.6 kg | boneless breast of turkey, self-basting |
| 1 tsp | 5 mL | vegetable oil |

- This can be cooked from a frozen state or thawed.
- To thaw, leave turkey breast in unopened bag on tray in fridge for 48 hours.
- Preheat oven to 325°F (165°C).
- Remove outside netting and plastic wrap (**do not remove inside netting**).
- Place turkey in a roasting pan and brush with vegetable oil.
- Insert meat thermometer into middle of breast.
- Roast 2 - 2½ hours (thawed) or 3 - 4 hours (if frozen) or until meat thermometer reads 180°F (82°C) (when turkey is light golden brown, cover lightly with foil to prevent burning).
- Remove from oven and let stand 15 minutes; remove netting and skin, slice and serve on a warm platter.

DID YOU KNOW?

Today's bride chooses her bouquet carefully, selecting flowers for their fragrance and beauty. At one time, she had far less choice - the bouquet she carried was stalks of grain which were supposed to symbolize fruitfulness.

STUFFING

1½ cups	375 mL	chopped onion
½ cup	125 mL	butter or margarine
2 tsp	10 mL	poultry seasoning
1 tsp	5 mL	seasoning salt
7 cups	1.75 L	coarse bread crumbs
1 cup	250 mL	milk (approximately)
1	1	poultry stuffing bag

- Preheat oven to 325°F (165°C).
- In a medium saucepan, over medium heat, saute onion in butter or margarine for 2 minutes.
- Remove from heat and add poultry seasoning, salt, bread and enough milk to moisten; mix well until bread crumbs absorb moisture.
- Spoon stuffing **loosely** into bag and form a roll, tie ends.
- Wrap lightly in foil and place in a roasting pan; bake 1 hour.
- Remove from bag and place in a warm vegetable bowl to serve.

TURKEY GRAVY

¼ cup	60 mL	*turkey drippings
¼ cup	60 mL	all purpose flour
¼ oz	5 g	instant chicken bouillon
1½ cups	375 mL	water (approximately)
(to taste)		salt
(to taste)		pepper

- In a roasting pan or a large frying pan, over medium heat, blend turkey drippings with flour and chicken bouillon.
- Slowly add water, stirring until gravy reaches a pouring consistency; bring to a boil (if gravy is too thick, add extra water).
- Season with salt and pepper to taste.
- Put in a gravy boat and serve.

If there isn't enough turkey drippings, add butter or margarine.

P.S.
Turkey, stuffing, and gravy leftovers may be separately wrapped or covered and stored in the refrigerator for 1 - 2 days or frozen for longer storage.

MASHED POTATOES

8	8	large white potatoes
1 tsp	5 mL	salt
		hot water (to cover)
¼ cup	60 mL	butter or margarine
1 cup	250 mL	sour cream
1 tsp	5 mL	salt
¼ tsp	1.2 mL	pepper

- Peel and quarter potatoes.
- In a large saucepan, over high heat, bring potatoes to a boil in salted water.
- Reduce heat to medium/low, cover and cook 40 minutes or until fork-tender; drain.
- Mash well with a potato masher; add remaining ingredients and mash well again.
- Serve in a warm vegetable bowl.

P.S.
Mashed Potatoes can be made ahead, stored in the fridge and reheated before serving; if you choose this method, you will need to allow 30 - 45 minutes for reheating in a preheated oven at 325°F (165°C).

SCALLOPED CORN

2	2	large eggs
3 tbsp	45 mL	all purpose flour
20 oz	568 mL	canned creamed corn
12 oz	341 mL	canned mexicorn, drained
⅔ cup	165 mL	milk
½ cup	125 mL	grated mild cheddar cheese
1 tsp	5 mL	salt
⅛ tsp	.6 mL	pepper

- Preheat oven to 325°F (165°C).
- In a medium mixing bowl, fork-beat eggs.
- With a wire whisk, blend in flour and then mix in remaining ingredients.
- Pour into a large greased casserole and bake 1½ hours or until set.
- Serve hot.

CRANBERRY SALAD

3 oz	85 g	raspberry jelly powder
1 cup	250 mL	boiling water
½ cup	125 mL	cold water
14 oz	398 mL	canned crushed pineapple, drained
½ cup	125 mL	canned whole cranberry sauce
¼ cup	60 mL	pecan pieces

- In a medium mixing bowl, dissolve jelly powder in boiling water.
- Add cold water and chill 45 minutes or until slightly thickened.
- Add remaining ingredients and stir to distribute well.
- Pour into a pretty serving bowl or mold and chill until set.

P.S.
Leftover cranberry can be used in Cranberry Squares, see Something Special - Coffee and Dessert, page 129.

ICED TEA

6 tbsp	90 mL	iced tea mix
5 cups	1.25 L	cold water
		ice
6	6	lemon slices

- In a large water pitcher, dissolve iced tea mix in water and refrigerate until required.
- To serve, fill 6 tall glasses with ice and pour tea over; garnish each with a lemon slice.

P.S.
For best results, make sure the glasses are filled with ice.

BE TO HIS VIRTUES VERY KIND;
BE TO HIS FAULTS VERY BLIND.

FROSTY PUMPKIN PIE

1½ cups	375 mL	graham crumbs
1 cup	250 mL	packed brown sugar
3 tbsp	45 mL	melted butter
8 oz	227 mL	canned pumpkin
½ tsp	2.5 mL	salt
½ tsp	2.5 mL	ground cinnamon
½ tsp	2.5 mL	ground ginger
¼ tsp	1.2 mL	ground nutmeg
2 cups	500 mL	vanilla ice cream, slightly softened
2 cups	500 mL	*whipped cream

- In a small mixing bowl, combine graham crumbs, half the sugar and the melted butter.
- Firmly press mixture into the bottom and sides of a 9" (23 cm) pie plate and freeze 30 minutes or until firm.
- In a medium mixing bowl, with mixer at medium speed, beat remaining sugar, pumpkin, salt, spices, and ice cream for 2 minutes or until smooth.
- Pour into crust and freeze at least 4 hours, covering with plastic wrap when filling is firm.
- **Thaw 45 minutes** and top with whipped cream just before serving.

See Sweet Things - Whipped Cream, page 105.

P.S.
Leftover pumpkin can be used in Pumpkin Slice, see Something Special - Coffee and Dessert, page 131.

48 hours ahead	- thaw **Turkey** in fridge
day before or early in day	- make **Frosty Pumpkin Pie**
early in day	- make **Cranberry Salad**
2½ hours ahead (thawed)	- place **Turkey Breast** in oven
1½ hours ahead	- place **Scalloped Corn** in oven
1 hour ahead	- place **Stuffing** in oven
	- put **Potatoes** on to cook
	- make **Iced Tea**
10 minutes ahead	- make **Gravy**

GOING SHOPPING

3½ lbs	1.6 kg	boneless breast of turkey, self-basting
20 oz	568 mL	canned creamed corn
14 oz	398 mL	canned crushed pineapple
12 oz	341 mL	canned mexicorn
8 oz	227 mL	canned pumpkin
4 oz	125 mL	canned whole cranberry sauce
5¼ oz	149 g	coarse bread crumbs
2	2	eggs (large)
8 oz	250 mL	heavy or whipping cream
1	1	lemon
1½ oz	42 g	mild cheddar cheese
4½ oz	128 g	onion
3 oz	85 g	raspberry jelly powder
8 oz	250 mL	sour cream
1 pt	500 mL	vanilla ice cream
8	8	white potatoes (large)

<u>Check Your Shelves For</u>:

all purpose flour	milk
brown sugar	pecan pieces
butter and/or margarine	pepper
graham crumbs	poultry seasoning
granulated sugar	poultry stuffing bag
ground cinnamon	salt
ground ginger	seasoning salt
ground nutmeg	vanilla
iced tea mix	vegetable oil
instant chicken bouillon	

SOMETHING SPECIAL

VALENTINE'S DAY   Serves 2

Valentine's day - a day to say "I Love You". And what better way than with a meal sure to impress that special person in your life.

LETTUCE ALONE SALAD
4	4	small lettuce wedges

- Remove outer leaves from a small firm head of lettuce and cut four 1" (2.5 cm) wedges from it.
- Rinse each wedge and chill at least 30 minutes or until required.
- To serve, place 2 wedges on each of 2 small plates and top with dressing (below).

DRESSING
¼ cup	60 mL	mayonnaise
4 tsp	20 mL	liquid honey
½ tsp	2.5 mL	red wine vinegar
½ tsp	2.5 mL	sesame seeds

- In a small bowl, combine all ingredients; mix well and refrigerate until required.

BAKED POTATOES
2	2	medium baker potatoes
		vegetable oil
2 tbsp	30 mL	butter or margarine
2 tbsp	30 mL	sour cream
½ tsp	2.5 mL	freeze-dried chives

- Preheat oven to 425°F (215°C).
- Wash potatoes, pat dry and rub with vegetable oil.
- Wrap each potato in foil and bake 1 hour or until fork-tender.
- When ready to serve, remove potatoes from foil, slash tops and squeeze to partially open; dot with butter or margarine, top with sour cream and sprinkle with chives.

PEPPERCORN STEAK

1½ tbsp	22.5 mL	green peppercorn sauce mix
2 tsp	10 mL	water (approximately)
2 tsp	10 mL	red wine vinegar
¼ cup	60 mL	heavy or whipping cream
2	2	beef tenderloin steaks

- Preheat broiler, if manufacturer directs.
- In a small saucepan, over medium heat, combine peppercorn sauce mix, water, vinegar and cream.
- Cook and stir until sauce comes to a boil; reduce heat to low and simmer 3 minutes.
- Remove from heat, cover to keep warm.
- Put steaks on rack in broiling pan and place on top shelf of oven.
- Broil to desired taste (rare - 7 minutes each side, medium - 8 minutes each side, well done - 10 minutes each side); place on warm plates.
- Pour peppercorn sauce over steaks (if sauce is too thick to pour, add a little more water and mix well); serve immediately.

CHEESE TOAST

1	1	large oval bun
2 tbsp	30 mL	butter or margarine, melted
½ cup	125 mL	grated mild cheddar cheese

- Preheat oven to 350°F (180°C).
- Angle cut bun in 1" (2.5 cm) slices; dip top of each slice into melted butter and sprinkle with cheese.
- Place on a pizza pan, cheese side up, and bake 7 minutes.
- Serve warm.

P.S.

If making cheese toast as part of this complete meal, it can be put in the oven beneath the broiling pan and baked 10 minutes while steak is broiling.

ZUCCHINI AND RED PEPPER

1	1	small red pepper, seeds removed
1	1	small zucchini
1 tbsp	15 mL	vegetable oil

- Preheat broiler, if manufacturer directs.
- Cut pepper and zucchini into ¼" (6 mm) slices.
- Toss with oil and place on broiler pan.
- Broil 3 minutes or until tender and lightly browned.
- Serve as side vegetables.

RASPBERRY KISS

Toast your truelove with this attractive drink.

24 oz	660 mL	gingerale
1¼ tsp	6.2 mL	raspberry flavor crystals
2	2	red maraschino cherries
2	2	toothpicks with frills

- Chill gingerale 1 hour; pour into 2 tall glasses.
- Stir in raspberry flavor crystals.
- Spear the maraschino cherries with toothpicks and place 1 in each glass.

DID YOU KNOW?

Toasting is thought to have come from an old French custom. During the wedding dinner, two goblets would each have a small square of baked bread placed in the bottom and filled with the couple's favorite beverage. The bride and groom would then raise their glasses to each other and begin to drink. Tradition has it that the first to drain the glass and get the "toast" would be the ruler of the home.

Although no one is sure how the custom of exchanging valentines began, by the 18th century it was very popular.

The heart, a symbol of love since early Roman times, is often used to express affection. Give your sweetheart a heart-shaped valentine this year, one you make yourself.

GINGERBREAD VALENTINE (pictured on page 89)

3 tbsp	45 mL	butter, softened
¼ cup	60 mL	packed brown sugar
¼ cup	60 mL	fancy molasses
¾ cup	185 mL	all purpose flour
½ tsp	2.5 mL	baking soda
¼ tsp	1.2 mL	ground cinnamon
½ tsp	2.5 mL	ground ginger
⅛ tsp	.6 mL	salt
1 tsp	5 mL	water
(optional)		creamy frosting
(optional)		sugar decorations

- Preheat oven to 375°F (190°C).
- In a small mixing bowl, with mixer at medium speed, cream butter and sugar together.
- Add molasses, flour, soda, cinnamon, ginger, salt and water; continue mixing for 2 minutes or until well blended.
- Press evenly into a non-stick heart shaped cake pan.
- Bake 8 - 10 minutes or until lightly browned around the edges (top will still feel slightly springy to the touch).
- Cool completely; gently loosen and remove from pan.
- Frost and decorate with sugar decorations (if desired) to make your own special valentine greeting.

P.S.
If making your valentine the day before, it will keep better stored in a plastic container until required.

day before or early in day	- make **Gingerbread Valentine**
early in day	- prepare **Salad** and **Dressing**
80 minutes ahead	- place **Potatoes** in oven
	- prepare **Raspberry Kiss**
20 minutes ahead	- prepare **Sauce** for steaks
16 minutes ahead (medium)	- broil **Steaks**
10 minutes ahead	- place **Cheese Toast** in oven
3 minutes ahead	- broil **Zucchini** and **Red Pepper**

GOING SHOPPING

2	2	baker potatoes (medium)
12 oz	341 g	beef tenderloin steaks
24 oz	660 mL	gingerale
2 oz	60 mL	heavy or whipping cream
1	1	lettuce head (small, firm)
1½ oz	42 g	mild cheddar cheese
1	1	oval bun (large)
1	1	red pepper (small)
1 oz	30 mL	sour cream
1	1	zucchini (small)

Check Your Shelves For:

all purpose flour	liquid honey
baking soda	mayonnaise
brown sugar	raspberry flavor crystals
butter and/or margarine	red maraschino cherries
creamy frosting (optional)	red wine vinegar
fancy molasses	salt
freeze-dried chives	sesame seeds
green peppercorn sauce mix	sugar decorations (optional)
ground cinnamon	toothpicks with frills
ground ginger	vegetable oil

NOTES

INDEX

Acorn Squash, 33
Almond Ice Cream, 93
Ants on a Log, 31
Apple
  in a Pie, 93
  Nut Rice, 111
  Pan Fried, 101
  Pancakes, 50
  sauce, 94

Bacon, 67
Baked Ham, 134
Baked Potatoes, 143
Banana Custard, 94
Bavarian Stew, 74
Bean(s)
  Salad, 123
  Saucy, 76
Beef
  Burger Barbecue, 44
  Cabbage Rolls, 121
  Chuckwagon Dinner, 62
  Gravy, 116
  Meat Sauce, 22
  Peppercorn Steak, 144
  Planned Over Chili, 80
  Roast Beef, 115
  Roast Ribbons, 40
Beets 'a la Orange, 117
Black Forest Impression, 95
Blueberry Cobbler, 95
Bread Pudding, 96
Broccoli Crisps, 111
Broiled Lobster Tails, 112
Burger Barbecue, 44

Cabbage
  and Apple Mix, 85
  Rolls, 121

Carrot(s)
  Cake, 118
  Nippy, 123
  /Raisin Salad, 27
Casseroles
  Bavarian Stew, 74
  Chinese Chicken, 68
  Chuckwagon Dinner, 62
  Ham and Potato, 26
  Planned Over Chili, 80
  Perogie, 122
  Tasty Tuna, 46
Cheese
  Cakes, Creamy Chocolate, 97
  Cakes, Hawaiian, 98
  Rolls, 61
  Toast, 144
Chicken
  Chinese, 68
  Crunchy, 20
  Mexican, 42
  Royale, 84
  Wings, 56
Chili, Planned over, 80
Chinese Chicken, 68
Chocolate Fondue, 127
Christmas Light Cookies, 96
Christmas Torte, 124
Chuckwagon Dinner, 62
Coconut Cream Bake, 97
Coffee
  Delicious, 87
  Drip Type, 128
Corn Cobs, 78
Crab Melt, 64
Cranberry
  Salad, 140
  Squares, 129
Creamy Broccoli Soup, 60

Creamy Chocolate Cheesecakes, 97
Croissants, Stuffed, 48
Crunchy Chicken, 20
Crusty Bun Bowls, 81

Delicious Coffee, 87
Desserts
  Almond Ice Cream, 93
  Apple in a Pie, 93
  Applesauce, 94
  Banana Custard, 94
  Black Forest Impression, 95
  Blueberry Cobbler, 95
  Bread Pudding, 96
  Carrot Cake, 118
  Chocolate Fondue, 127
  Christmas Light Cookies, 96
  Christmas Torte, 124
  Coconut Cream Bake, 97
  Cranberry Squares, 129
  Creamy Chocolate Cheesecakes, 97
  Frosty Pumpkin Pie, 141
  Gingerbread Valentine, 146
  Gingersnap Log, 98
  Hawaiian Cheesecakes, 98
  Ice Cream Parfait, 112
  Iced Popcorn, 58
  Krispie Rainbow Treats, 99
  Malt, 99
  Maple Pears, 100
  Mystery Confection, 100
  Nut Clusters, 132
  Palm Sundae, 135
  Pan Fried Apple, 101
  Peach Delight, 101
  Peanut Butter Crunch, 102
  Pineapple Delight, 130
  Puffed Wheat Squares, 102
  Pumpkin Slice, 131

Desserts (continued)
  Raisin Pears, 103
  Raspberry Surprise, 103
  S'mores, 104
  Strawberry Deluxe, 104
  Sundae Special, 105
  Whipped Cream, 105
  Dumplings, 75

Egg(s)
  Marbled, 133
  Salmon Scramble, 28
  Vegetarian Quiche, 38

French Toast, 66
Fresh Strawberries, 86
Fries, 83
Frosty Pumpkin Pie, 141
Fruit
  Bowl, 21
  Fresh Strawberries, 86
  'n Dip, 49
  Mandarin Fruit Salad, 68

Garden Salad, 30
Gingerbread Valentine, 146
Gingersnap Log, 98
Glazed Onions, 115
Gravy
  Beef, 116
  Turkey, 138
Green Beans Supreme, 135

Ham
  Baked, 134
  and Potato Casserole, 26
  Hawaiian Cheesecakes, 98
  Hobos, 30

Index (continued)

Ice Cream Parfait, 112
Iced Popcorn, 58
Iced Tea, 140

Kabobs, Veal, 24
Krispie Rainbow Treats, 99

Lettuce Alone Salad, 143
Little Loaves, 78
Lobster, Broiled Tails, 112

Malt, 99
Mandarin Fruit Salad, 68
Maple Pears, 100
Marbled Eggs, 133
Mashed Potatoes, 139
Meat Sauce, 22
Mexican Chicken, 42
Mystery Confection, 100

New Potatoes, 116
Nippy Carrots, 123
Nut Clusters, 132

Onions, Glazed, 115
Orange Sauce, 66

Palm Sundae, 135
Pan Fried Apple, 101
Pancakes, Apple, 50
Parsley Potatoes, 20
Pasta
  Spaghetti, 23
  Spiral, 65
  Vermicelli, 40
Peach Delight, 101
Peanut Butter Crunch, 102
Peppercorn Steak, 144
Perogie Casserole, 122
Pineapple Delight, 130

Pizza, 58
Planned Over Chili, 80
Potato(es)
  Baked, 143
  Fries, 83
  Mashed, 139
  New, 116
  Parsley, 20
  Sweet, 134
Pudding, Bread, 96
Puffed Wheat Squares, 102
Pumpkin Slice, 131

Quiche, Vegetarian, 38

Raisin Pears, 103
Raisin Tea Biscuits, 86
Raspberry Kiss, 145
Raspberry Surprise, 103
Rice
  Apple Nut, 111
  Steamed, 25
  Vegetable, 57
Roast
  Beef, 115
  Ribbons, 40
  Turkey Breast, 137

Salad
  Bean, 123
  Cabbage and Apple Mix, 85
  Carrot/Raisin, 27
  Cranberry, 140
  Fruit Bowl, 21
  Fruit 'n Dip, 49
  Garden, 30
  Lettuce Alone, 143
  Mandarin Fruit, 68
  Spinach, 39
Salmon Scramble, 28

Index (continued)

Sauce
  Orange, 66
  Sour Cream, 29
  Sweet & Sour, 56
  Tangy, 51
  White, 48
Saucy Beans, 76
Sausage(s)
  Bavarian Stew, 74
  Small, 50
  Ukrainian, 122
Scalloped Corn, 139
Seafood
  Broiled Lobster Tails, 112
  Crab Melt, 64
  Salmon Scramble, 28
  Shrimp Sandwiches, 82
  Tasty Tuna, 46
Shrimp Sandwiches, 82
Small Sausages, 50
S'mores, 104
Soup, Creamy Broccoli, 60
Sour Cream Sauce, 29
Spaghetti, 23
Spinach Salad, 39
Spiral Pasta, 65
Squash, Acorn, 33
Steak, Peppercorn, 144
Steamed Rice, 25
Stew, Bavarian, 74
Strawberry Deluxe, 104
Stuffed Croissants, 48
Stuffing, 138
Sundae Special, 105
Sweet & Sour Sauce, 56
Sweet Potatoes, 134

Tangy Sauce, 51

Tasty Tuna, 46
Tea, Iced, 140
Tomato
  Cups, 79
  Wedges, 47
Turkey
  Gravy, 138
  Roast Breast, 137
  Roll-ups, 32
  Wiener Wraps, 76

Ukrainian Sausage, 122

Veal
  Kabobs, 24
  Little Loaves, 78
Vegetable(s)
  Acorn Squash, 33
  Beets 'a la Orange, 117
  Broccoli Crisps, 111
  Corn Cobs, 78
  Glazed Onions, 115
  Green Beans Supreme, 135
  Nippy Carrots, 123
  Rice, 57
  Scalloped Corn, 139
  Tomato Cups, 79
  Zucchini and Red Pepper, 145
Vegetarian Quiche, 38
Vermicelli, 40

Whipped Cream, 105
White Sauce, 48
Wiener Wraps, 76

Yorkshire Pudding, 117

Zucchini and Red Pepper, 145

GIVE *Just Married Cookbook* TO A FRIEND!

NAME_____

STREET_____

CITY_____ PROV/STATE_____

COUNTRY_____ POSTAL/ZIP CODE_____

Please send _____ copies of Just Married Cookbook at $14.95 **each**, plus $2.00 **each** for postage and handling:

NUMBER OF BOOKS_____ X $14.95 = $ _____
ADD $2.00 POSTAGE AND HANDLING PER COPY____ = $ _____
SUBTOTAL_____ $ _____
IN CANADA, ADD 7% G.S.T.____ (SUBTOTAL X .07) = $ _____
TOTAL ENCLOSED_____ $ _____

U.S. or International Orders payable in U.S. funds

Make cheque or money order payable to: Just Married Cookbook
P. O. Box 431, Station M
Calgary, Alberta, Canada T2P 2J1

PRICE SUBJECT TO CHANGE WITHOUT PRIOR NOTICE - SORRY, NO C.O.D.'S

GIVE *Just Married Cookbook* TO A FRIEND!

NAME_____

STREET_____

CITY_____ PROV/STATE_____

COUNTRY_____ POSTAL/ZIP CODE_____

Please send _____ copies of Just Married Cookbook at $14.95 **each**, plus $2.00 **each** for postage and handling:

NUMBER OF BOOKS_____ X $14.95 = $ _____
ADD $2.00 POSTAGE AND HANDLING PER COPY____ = $ _____
SUBTOTAL_____ $ _____
IN CANADA, ADD 7% G.S.T.____ (SUBTOTAL X .07) = $ _____
TOTAL ENCLOSED_____ $ _____

U.S. or International Orders payable in U.S. funds

Make cheque or money order payable to: Just Married Cookbook
P. O. Box 431, Station M
Calgary, Alberta, Canada T2P 2J1

PRICE SUBJECT TO CHANGE WITHOUT PRIOR NOTICE - SORRY, NO C.O.D.'S

THIS PAGE MAY BE COPIED

GIVE *Just Married Cookbook* TO A FRIEND!

NAME_____

STREET_____

CITY_____ PROV/STATE_____

COUNTRY_____ POSTAL/ZIP CODE_____

Please send _____ copies of Just Married Cookbook at $14.95 **each**, plus $2.00 **each** for postage and handling:

NUMBER OF BOOKS_____ X $14.95 = $ _____
ADD $2.00 POSTAGE AND HANDLING PER COPY____ = $ _____
SUBTOTAL_____ $ _____
IN CANADA, ADD 7% G.S.T.____ (SUBTOTAL X .07) = $ _____
TOTAL ENCLOSED_____ $ _____

U.S. or International Orders payable in U.S. funds

Make cheque or money order payable to: Just Married Cookbook
P. O. Box 431, Station M
Calgary, Alberta, Canada T2P 2J1

PRICE SUBJECT TO CHANGE WITHOUT PRIOR NOTICE - SORRY, NO C.O.D.'S

GIVE *Just Married Cookbook* TO A FRIEND!

NAME_____

STREET_____

CITY_____ PROV/STATE_____

COUNTRY_____ POSTAL/ZIP CODE_____

Please send _____ copies of Just Married Cookbook at $14.95 **each**, plus $2.00 **each** for postage and handling:

NUMBER OF BOOKS_____ X $14.95 = $ _____
ADD $2.00 POSTAGE AND HANDLING PER COPY____ = $ _____
SUBTOTAL_____ $ _____
IN CANADA, ADD 7% G.S.T.____ (SUBTOTAL X .07) = $ _____
TOTAL ENCLOSED_____ $ _____

U.S. or International Orders payable in U.S. funds

Make cheque or money order payable to: Just Married Cookbook
P. O. Box 431, Station M
Calgary, Alberta, Canada T2P 2J1

PRICE SUBJECT TO CHANGE WITHOUT PRIOR NOTICE - SORRY, NO C.O.D.'S

THIS PAGE MAY BE COPIED